Paul Carter

English
with ... games
and activities

© 2004 - ELI s.r.l.
P.O. Box 6 - Recanati - Italy
Tel. +39 071 75 07 01 - Fax +39 071 97 78 51
www.elionline.com
e-mail: info@elionline.com

Illustrated by Roberto Battestini
Graphic design by Studio Cornell sas
English version by Paul Carter and Maria Cleary

Adapted from *L'Italiano con giochi e attività*
by Federica Colombo

All rights reserved.
No part of this publication may be reproduced in any form or by any means or for any purpose without the prior permission of ELI.

Printed in Italy - Tecnostampa Recanati - 04.83.087.0

ISBN - 978-88-536-0001-1

Introduction

English with games and activities has been devised for students of varying ages and competence levels, studying English as a foreign language.

The series, based on a functional communicative approach, is made up of 3 books in order to help students gradually learn basic English vocabulary and grammar.

There are **14 units** in each book, each one covering a commonly used lexical area.

English with games and activities – intermediate level introduces many new themes and takes a closer look at themes that have been covered in the previous two **English with games and activities** books.

There are about 20 illustrated words on the first page of each unit. These words are then used on the following five pages in various **games and activities** such as crosswords, wordsearches, anagrams, etc.

Basic grammar points are introduced in each unit and revised throughout the book.

The **Answers** to all the exercises can be found at the back of the book making this book ideal for self-study.

Parts of the body II

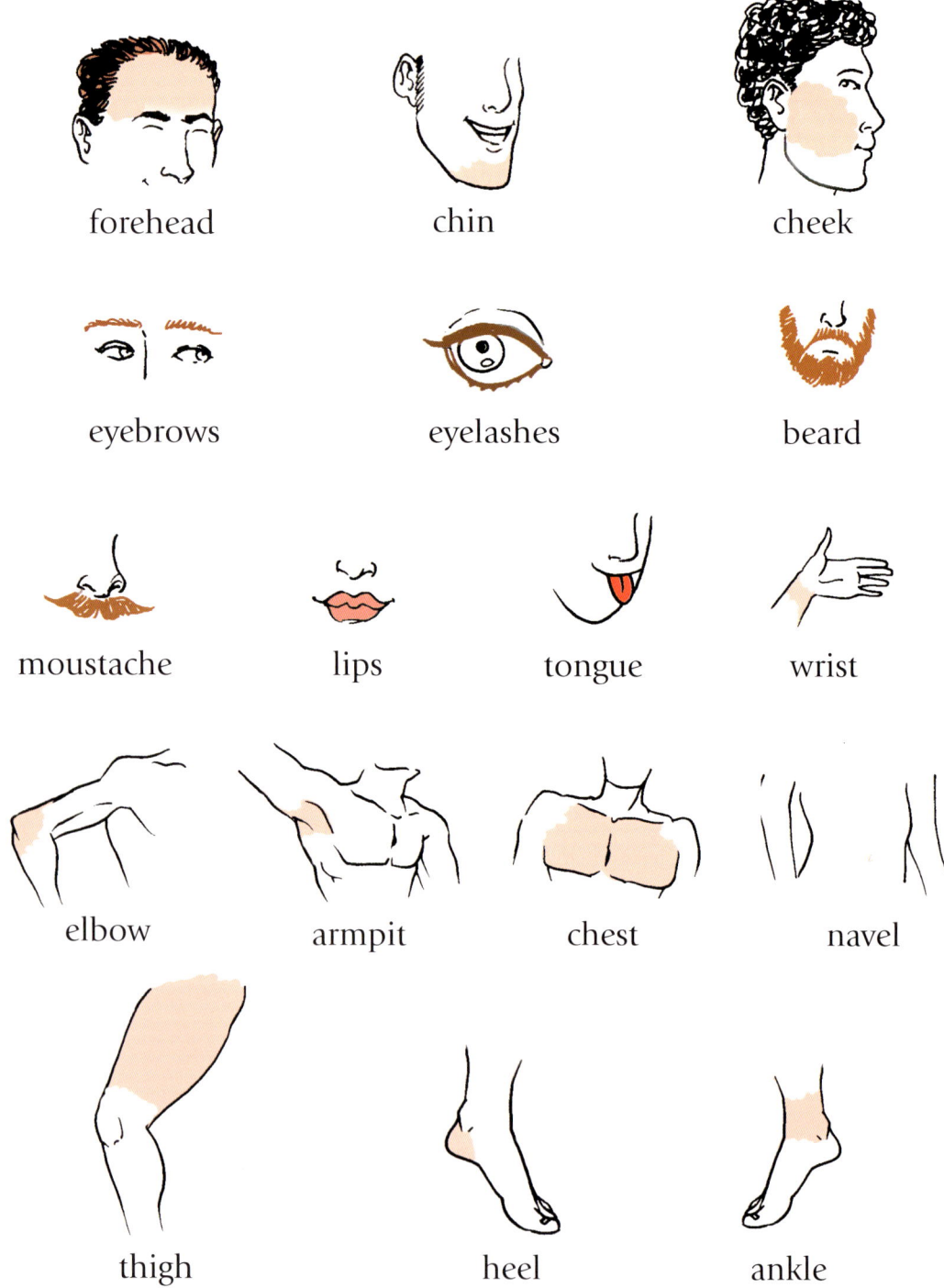

1 Faces. Look and write.

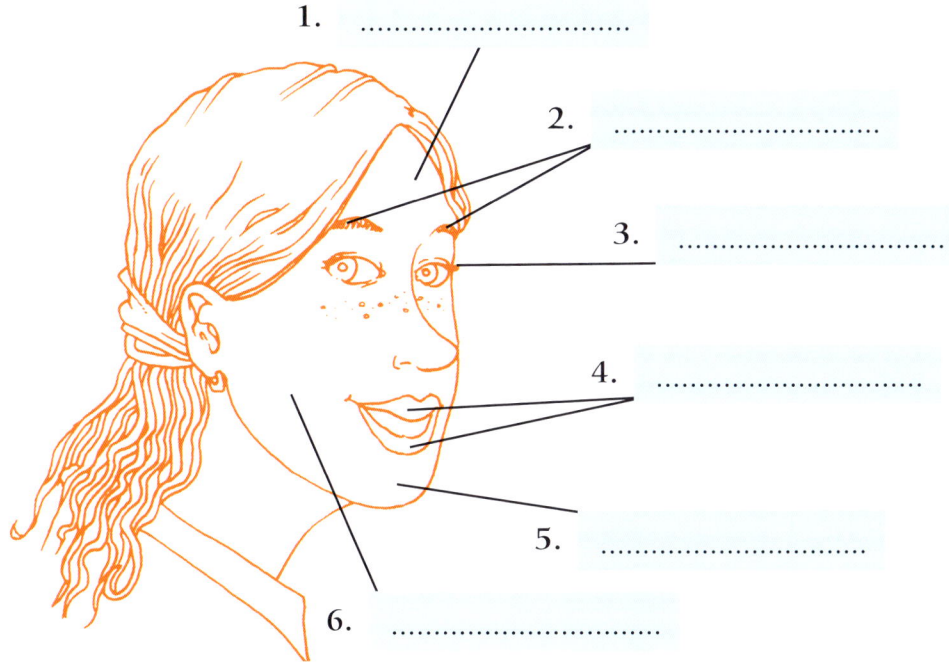

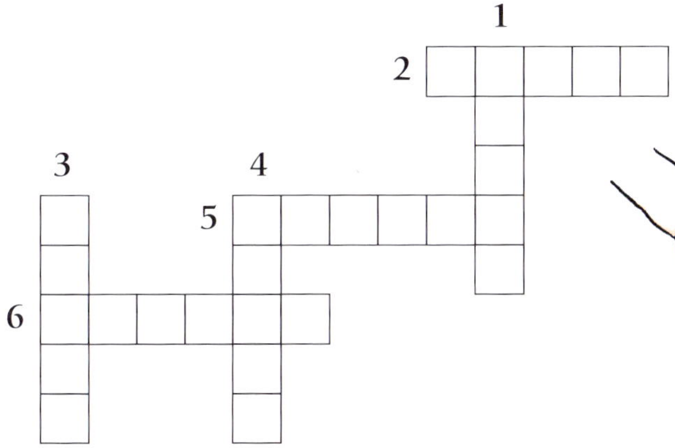

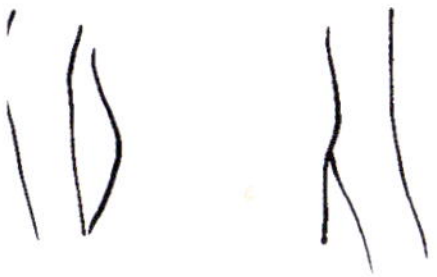

1. ....

2. ....

3. ....

4. ....

5. ....

6. ....

2 Body cross. Look then write the words in the crossword grid.

1

2

3

4

5

6

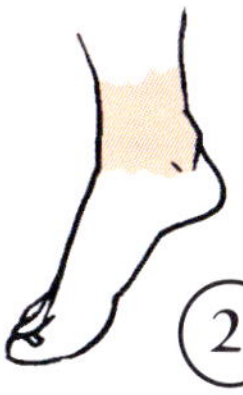

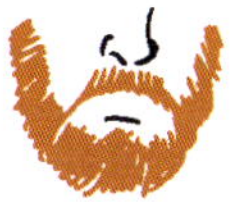

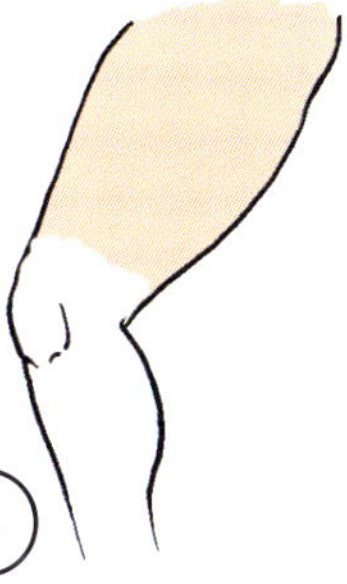

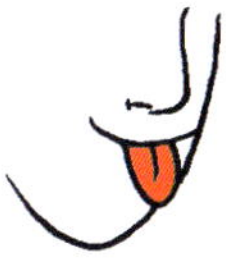

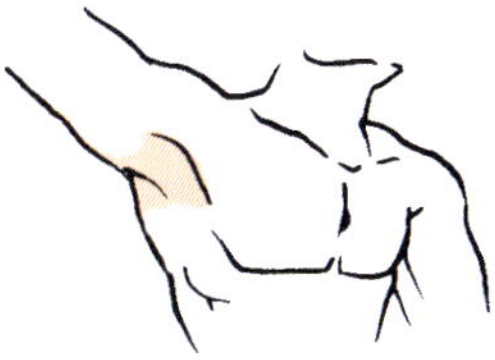

grammar

*We compare two people or things with the **comparative form + than**.*
Her eyes are **bigger than** John's eyes.

*We can also use **(not) as . . . as**.*
John's eyes **aren't as big as** Sally's eyes.

*If the noun is the same we can use **one** or **ones**.*
John's eyes are smaller than Sally's **ones**.

We compare three or more things with the superlative form.
Bill's chin is **long**. Harry's one is **longer**. But John's one is the **longest**.

Adjective	Comparative	Superlative
Adjectives with one syllable short	shorter	shortest
Adjectives with one vowel and one consonant big	bigger	biggest
Adjectives with two syllables supple	more supple	most supple
Adjectives with two syllables ending in -y shiny	shinier	shiniest
Adjectives with three syllables flexible	more flexible	most flexible

3 Look at the drawings and write the sentences using the comparative form.

1. Caroline's .... are (thin) .... than Sophie's ones

2. Phil's .... is (long) .... than John's one.

3. Anne's .... are (curly) .... than Karen's ones

4. Harry's .... is (pointy) .... than Richard's one.

5. Max's .... is (wrinkled) .... than Sam's one.

4 The most. Choose the best adjective then make the superlative form.

curly – flexible – pointy – red – smelly

1. Jim has the .... nose.
2. Caroline has the .... hair.
3. Susan has the .... cheeks.
4. Lou has the .... armpits.
5. Harry has the .... wrists.

5 What is it?

1. It's between your leg and your foot.
   ....
2. It's the part of your face under your mouth.
   ....
3. It's the part of your face above your eyebrows.
   ....
4. It's under your arm.
   ....
5. It's the hair above a man's mouth.
   ....
6. It's the hair on a man's chin.
   ....
7. It's in your mouth.
   ....
8. It's the top half of a leg.
   ....
9. It's between your arm and your hand.
   ....

6 Look at the drawings then match each idiom with the correct meaning.

1. To get something off your chest!   ☐ a. To keep quiet when you really want to talk.

2. To be head over heels in love.   ☐ b. To have enough space.

3. To keep your chin up!   ☐ c. To be completely in love.

4. To keep a stiff upper lip.   ☐ d. To ignore someone when they insult you.

5. To bite your tongue!   ☐ e. To talk about something that is important to you.

6. To raise people's eyebrows.   ☐ f. To stay calm in a difficult situation

7. To have enough elbow room.   ☐ g. To shock people.

8. To turn the other cheek.   ☐ h. To hide your feelings.

7 Who is it? Read the descriptions and decide who it is.

a. ☐

c. ☐

He has brown hair and a beard.
He has blue eyes and he wears glasses.
He has a long nose and red cheeks.
He has bushy eyebrows. Who is he?

b. ☐

d. ☐

8 Find the words. Find fifteen words from this unit in the wordsearch box. Use the remaining letters to complete the sentence.

```
M  O  U  S  T  A  C  H  E  A  C  T
T  H  E  Y  E  L  A  S  H  E  S  H
O  W  R  I  S  T  E  L  B  O  W  I
N  I  A  R  M  P  I  T  A  N  C  G
G  L  I  P  S  L  L  E  N  A  H  H
U  '  B  E  A  R  D  S  K  V  E  E
E  Y  E  B  R  O  W  S  L  E  S  E
F  O  R  E  H  E  A  D  E  L  T  L
```

Something you are not good at doing is called your _ _ _ _ _ _ _ _ _ heel.

Describe yourself to a friend.
Now describe your friend.
How are you different?

First aid

temperature

cough

cold

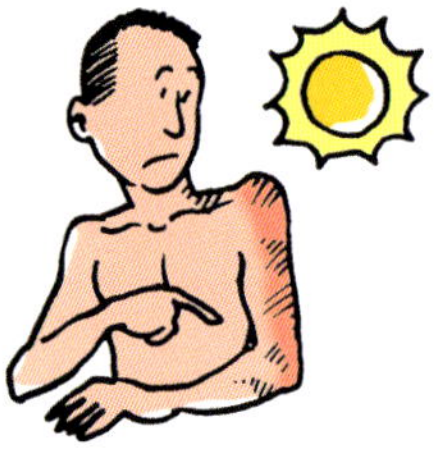

sunburn

sore throat

stomach ache

headache

toothache

ambulance

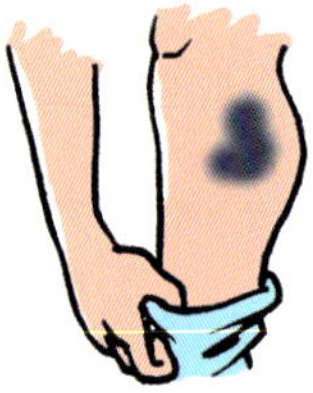

bruise

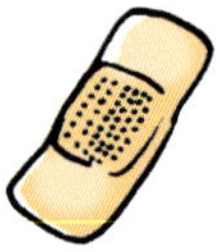

plaster

sling

bandage

nurse

hospital

doctor

chemist

medicine

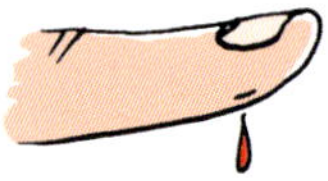

blood

1 Doctor! Doctor! I've got ... Match the words and the drawings.

1. ☐ a temperature
2. ☐ a cough
3. ☐ a cold
4. ☐ sunburn
5. ☐ a sore throat
6. ☐ a stomach ache
7. ☐ a headache
8. ☐ a toothache

a.
b.
c.
d.
e.
f.
g.
h.

2 Red cross. Look then write the words in the crossword grid.

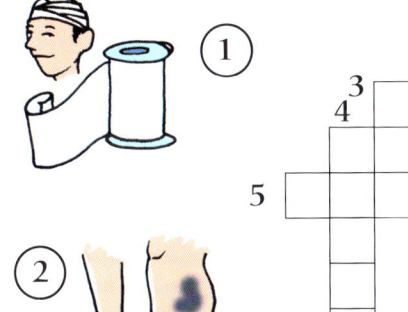

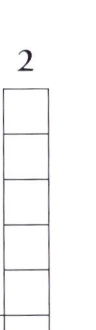

grammar

Past simple of 'be'

I was	I wasn't (was not)	Was I?
You were	You weren't	Were you
He was	He wasn't	Was he?
She was	She wasn't	Was she?
It was	It wasn't	Was it?
We were	We weren't	Were we?
You were	You weren't	Were you?
They were	They weren't	Were they?

Past simple of 'have'

I had	I didn't (did not) have	Did I have (had I)?
You had	You didn't have	Did you have?
He had	He didn't have	Did he have?
She had	She didn't have	Did she have?
It had	It didn't have	Did it have?
We had	We didn't have	Did we have?
You had	You didn't have	Did you have?
They had	They didn't have	Did they have?

We use the past simple for something that started and finished in the past.
Jane **had** a toothache.
Nick **was** ill.

3 What did they have? Look at the drawings and complete these sentences.

1. Chris .... a _ _ _ _ _.

2. .... Tony .... a _ _ _ _?

3. Michelle .... a _ _ _ _ _ _ _ _ _ _ _.

4. .... you .... a _ _ _ _ _ _ _ _ _?

4 Read then answer the questions.

1. Did Patricia have a headache?
   Yes, *she had a headache.* .

2. Was there much blood?
   No, ...

3. Did John have a temperature?
   No, ...

4. Was your throat sore?
   Yes, ...

5. Were his bruises big?
   Yes, ...

6. Did they have sunburn?
   Yes, ...

7. Did you have a toothache?
   No, ...

5 Find eight words from this unit in the wordsearch box. Use the remaining letters to complete the sentence.

T	E	M	P	E	R	A	T	U	R	E
C	F	M	E	D	I	C	I	N	E	I
O	C	T	B	A	N	D	A	G	E	F
U	O	I	D	B	L	O	O	D	D	L
G	L	T	O	O	T	H	A	C	H	E
H	D	H	E	A	D	A	C	H	E	E

If someone is healthy we can say they are as _ _ _ as a _ _ _ _ _ _.

6 Doctor's report. Look at the drawings and complete the doctor's report.

1. Mrs Brown .*had*........
   a ....

2. Her son, Jimmy, ...
   a ....

3. Susan Power was on holiday and she ....
   ....

4. Mr Wilson ....
   a ....

5. The twins ....
   ....

6. And me? At the end of the day I ....
   a ....

7 What is it? Read the descriptions then write what it is.

1. It's dangerous when it's high.

   ....

2. It's red and you can lose it if you have a bad accident.

   ....

3. You take it when you're sick.

   ....

4. If you have one you go to the dentist.

   ....

5. It's a place full of sick people.

   ....

6. If you break your arm you put it in this.

   ....

8 Do the crossword.

How do you feel?

How much?

ounce

pound
(1 pound = 16 ounces)

stone
(1 stone = 14 pounds)

teaspoon

dessertspoon

tablespoon

scales

can

box

tin

tea bag

bottle

jar

packet

carton

tube

bar

slice

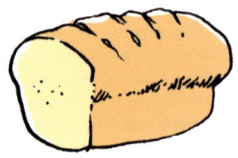
loaf

1. Big Bigger Biggest. Unscramble the words then put them in order from the smallest to the biggest.

a. ☐ .... DONUP

b. ☐ .... ONEST

c. ☐ .... ENUCO

2. Put the food in the correct containers.

1. a box of   a. orangeade

2. a can of   b. yogurt

3. a tin of   c. jam

4. a bottle of   d. chocolates

5. a packet of   e. wine

6. a jar of   f. tuna

7. a carton of   g. crisps

grammar

Crisp *is countable.*
a crisp (one)   **some** crisps (more than one)
Tuna *is uncountable.*
some tuna
We make uncountable nouns countable by adding a unit.
A tin of tuna   **some tins of** tuna

We use **a lot of** *and* **lots of** *with both countable and uncountable nouns when there is a large quantity.*
a lot of crisps   **lots of** crisps
a lot of tuna   **lots of** tuna
We use **a few** *with countable nouns and* **a little** *with uncountable nouns when there is a small quantity.*
a few crisps
a little tuna
We may also use **not many** *with countable nouns and* **not much** *with uncountable nouns when there is a small quantity.*
not many crisps
not much tuna

3 Look at the drawings and use *a lot of, lots of, a few* and *a little* to write sentences.

  There are a few chips but there's a lot of salad.

 1. ....

 3. ....

 2. ....

 4. ....

4 What about you? Write how much you eat or drink of these things.

1. meat   ....
2. vegetables ....
3. cheese   ....
4. water   ....
5. fish   ....
6. eggs   ....
7. fruit   ....
8. pasta   ....
9. milk   ....
10. biscuits   ....

5 Write the correct unit in the recipe below.

Shortbread

1/2 .... of flour   4 .... of sugar

6 .... of butter   1/4 .... of salt

Now put the instructions in order to make your shortbread.

☐ a. Mark into eight portions.

☐ b. Roll the mixture into a circle.

☐ c. Rub the butter into the other ingredients until you have a smooth mixture.

☐ d. Bake in the oven at 160° C for 45 minutes.

6 The shopping list. Complete the list with the correct units.

a slice of cheese

1. .... cola
2. .... tuna
3. .... flour
4. .... pasta
5. .... toothpaste
6. .... juice
7. .... strawberry jam
8. .... bread

can
carton
jar
packet
loaf
pound
tin
tube
slice

7 What is it?

1. It's for drinks. It can be plastic or glass.
   It's a ....

2. It's small and made of metal.
   ....

3. It's small and made of paper.
   You put it in hot water to make a drink.
   ....

4. It's quite small and is made of glass.
   ....

5. It's long and thin and usually made of plastic.
   You squeeze it.
   ....

8 Do the crossword.

How many ounces are there in a stone?

In the garden

1 Do the crossword. Use the letters in the grey boxes to complete the quote from a famous poem by Robert Burns.

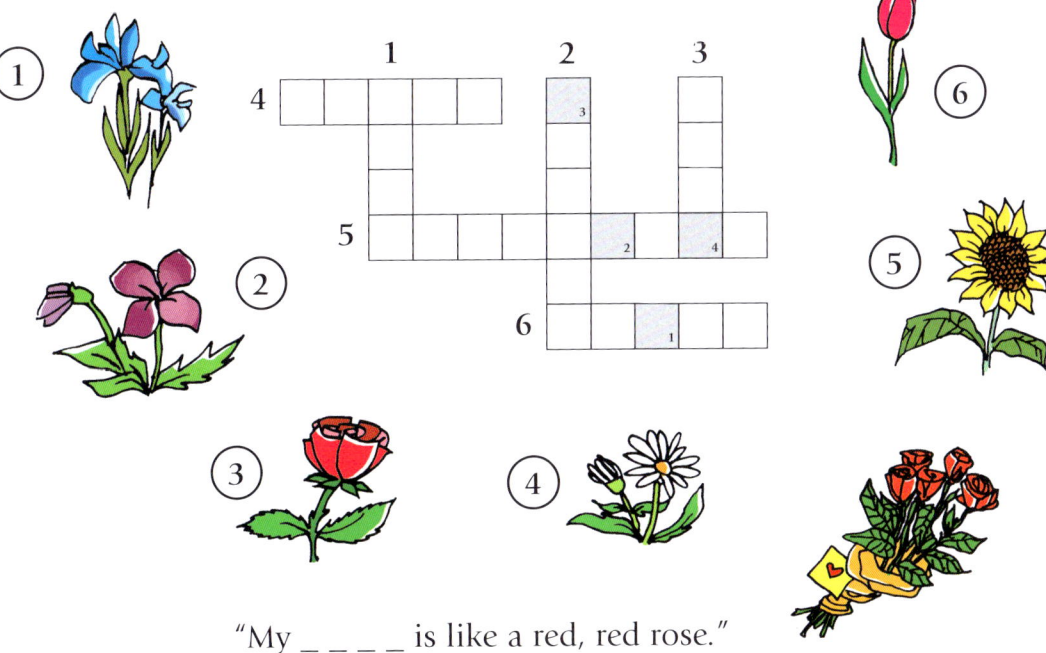

"My _ _ _ _ is like a red, red rose."
    1 2 3 4

2 Look and write the names in the grid. The letters in the grey boxes spell what you get when there are lots of these trees.

You find lots of these trees in a _ _ _ _ _ _.

grammar

We ask specific questions by putting question words before the interrogative form of the verb.

What is it? It's an oak tree.
Where do sunflowers grow? They grow in warm countries.
When do snowdrops grow? They grow in winter.

Question words:
What   Who
When   Why
Where   How

3 Complete the questions with the correct question words. Can you answer them?

What – When – Where – Why

1. .... colour are daffodils?
   ....

2. .... do tulips come from?
   ....
   ....

3. .... are roses traditional on Saint Valentine's Day?
   ....
   ....

4. .... do sunflowers grow?
   ....

4. Put the questions in the correct order. Answer them.

1. gives – Who – flowers – you ?
   ....
   ....

2. your – What – flowers – favourite – are ?
   ....
   ....

3. flowers – When – you – get – do ?
   ....
   ....

4. you – buy – flowers – do – Where ?
   ....
   ....

5. flowers – send – Why – you – do ?
   ....
   ....

5. What is it?

1. Its leaves are needles.
   ....

2. It is very tall and narrow.
   ....

3. Children play conkers with this nut.
   ....

4. It's got a very sad name.
   ....

5. It's a noble tree and acorns grow on it.
   ....

6 Poetry and plants. Complete these famous poems with the names of the correct flowers.

1. Ah ....! weary of time,
   Who countest the steps of the Sun:
   Seeking after that sweet golden clime
   Where the traveller's journey is done.
   William Blake

2. I wander'd lonely as a cloud
   That floats on high o'er vales and hills,
   When all at once I saw a crowd,
   A host of golden ....
   William Wordsworth

3. The .... but deceives;
   "He loves me not, he loves me well".
   One story no two .... tell.
   Helen Jackson

7 The meaning of flowers. Unscramble the flower names and discover their hidden meaning.

1. SAYID   Loyal love and innocence
                  ....

2. FALDOFID   Respect
                  ....

3. HODIRC   Maturity and charm
                  ....

4. TILOVE   Faithfulness and virtue
                  ....

5. PULTI   Luck
                  ....

6. SORE   Passion and love
                  ....

7. SIRI   Wisdom and hope
                  ....

8 What's in the garden? Write the names of the flowers and trees.

....

....

....

9 Find the names of the flowers and trees in the wordsearch box.
Use the remaining letters to complete the quote from Kahil Gibran.

```
W E E P I N G W I L L O W
C Y C L A M E N I R I S O
Y C H E S T N U T T R E R
P E S P S N O W D R O P C
R D A I S Y V I O L E T H
E F I R O E M T U L I P I
S U N F L O W E R O S E D
S S E D A F F O D I L A R
T H O A K S K B I R C H Y
```

_ _ _ _ _ are _ _ _ _ _ _ that the _ _ _ _ _
writes upon the _ _ _.
Kahil Gibran

What are your favourite flowers? Why?

Cars

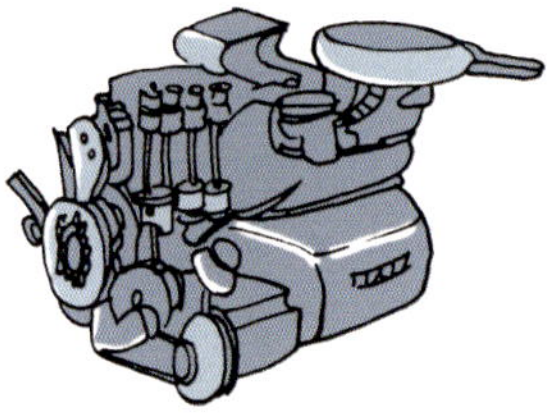

| engine |  door |  window |  seat |

| pedals |  steering wheel | 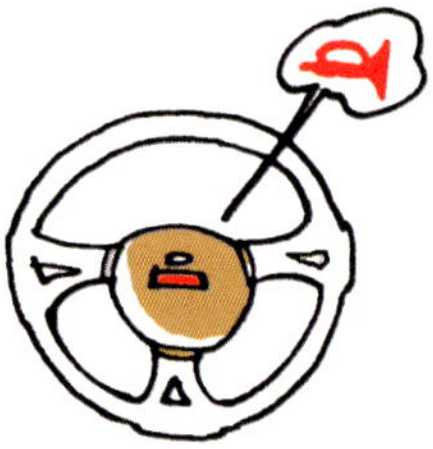 horn |  gear stick |

| rearview mirror |  seat belt |  windscreen | 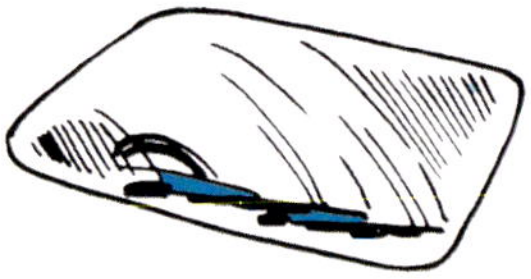 windscreen wiper |

| lights | 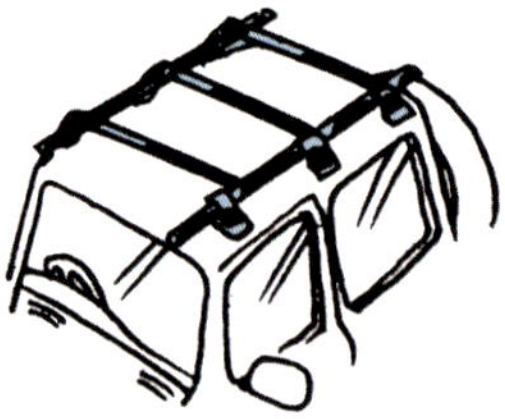 roof rack |  wheel |  jack |

| boot | number plate | 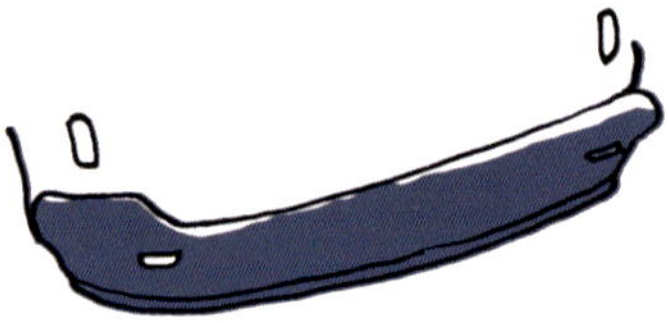 bumper |

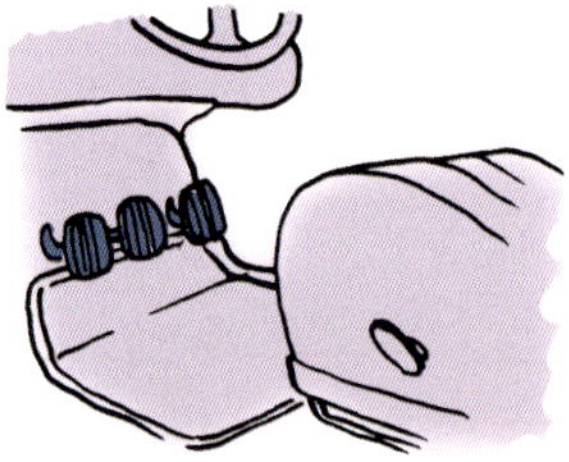

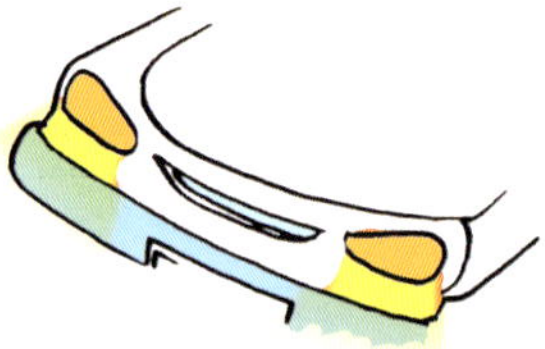

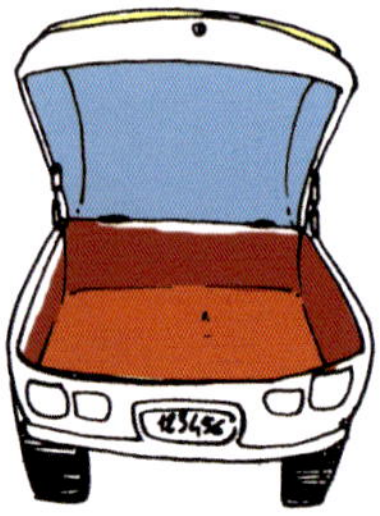

1 Match the actions with the car parts.

1. wind down   a. the steering wheel
2. turn on   b. the window
3. look in   c. the horn
4. close   d. the lights
5. put on   e. the rearview mirror
6. sound   f. the door
7. turn   g. the seat belt

2 Look at the drawing then write the names in the grid.

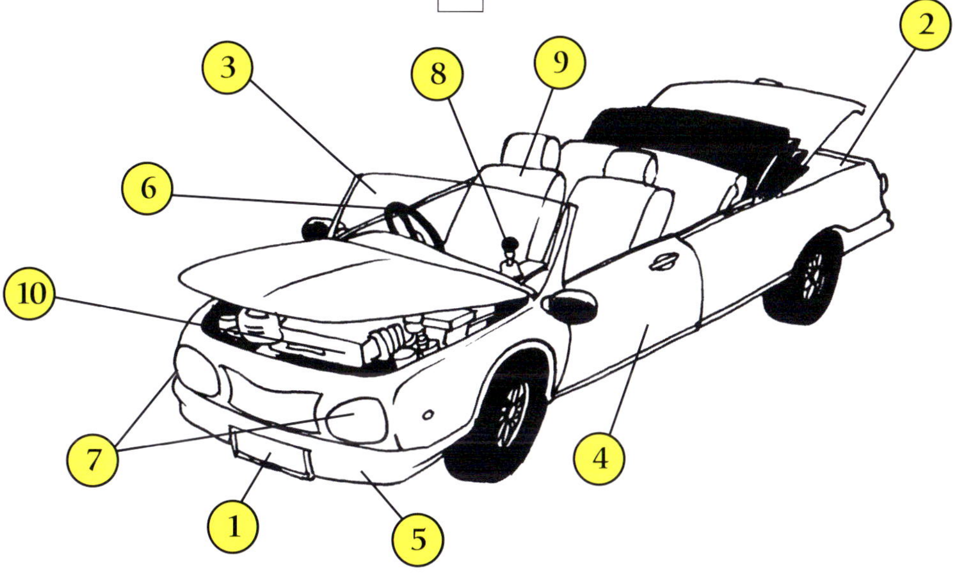

grammar

In English many verbs are formed with a verb + adverb. These verbs are called phrasal verbs. Sometimes the meaning is easy to understand but sometimes phrasal verbs can have a special meaning which is difficult to guess.

She **is putting on** her seat belt.
He **is getting into** the car.
Wind down the window please, it's very hot.

3 Write the words then complete these sentences with the correct phrasal verbs.

looks in – press down – put on – take off – turn on – wind up

1. When it's dark you .... the  ....

2. If you get a puncture you .... the  ....

3. When it's cold you .... the 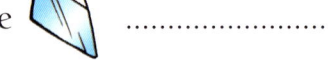 ....

4. You must .... your  ....

5. To go quickly and slowly you .... on the  ....

6. A good driver often .... the 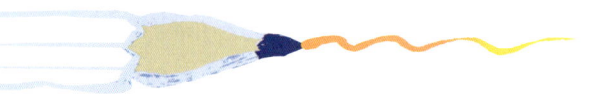 ....

grammar

*We use **must** for something that is necessary.*
***Must** is irregular: there is no 's' with he, she or it.*
*You do not use **to** after must.*

She **must** drive home.
I **must** wash my car.

4 Sally must go to the mechanic. Write the reasons why.

1. She must change the _ _ _ _ _ _ _ _ _ _ _.
2. She must check the _ _ _ _ _ _.
3. She must change the _ _ _ _ _.
4. She must get a new _ _ _ _ _.
5. She must fix the _ _ _ _ _ _ _ _ _ _ _.

5 Driving School. Can you answer the questions correctly?

1. You use it to change gear.
   - a. the gear stick
   - b. the pedal

2. You use it to carry large packages.
   - a. the jack
   - b. the roof rack

3. You use it to keep safe in the car.
   - a. the seat belt
   - b. the steering wheel

4. You use it to see when it's raining.
   - a. the bumper
   - b. the windscreen wiper

5. You use it to identify a car.
   - a. the roof rack
   - b. the number plate

6. You use it to change direction.
   - a. the wheel
   - b. the steering wheel

6 Look at the drawings then choose the correct sentence.

1. ☐ a. Can you wind down the window, please?
   ☐ b. Can you wind up the window, please?

2. ☐ a. Sound the horn because she's going slowly.
   ☐ b. Don't sound the horn! She's learning to drive.

3. ☐ a. There's lots of room in the boot.
   ☐ b. There isn't any room in the boot.

4. ☐ a. Can I move my seat back, please?
   ☐ b. Can I move my seat belt back, please?

7 Solve the riddles.

1. It's round. There's two on a bike and four on a car.
   It's a ....

2. It sounds like a shoe but you can put bags in it.
   It's a ....

3. It sounds like a man but it helps you when you have a puncture.
   It's a ....

4. There are two on a bull but in a car it makes a noise.
   It's a ....

8 Do the crossword. Then use the numbered letters to complete the sentence.

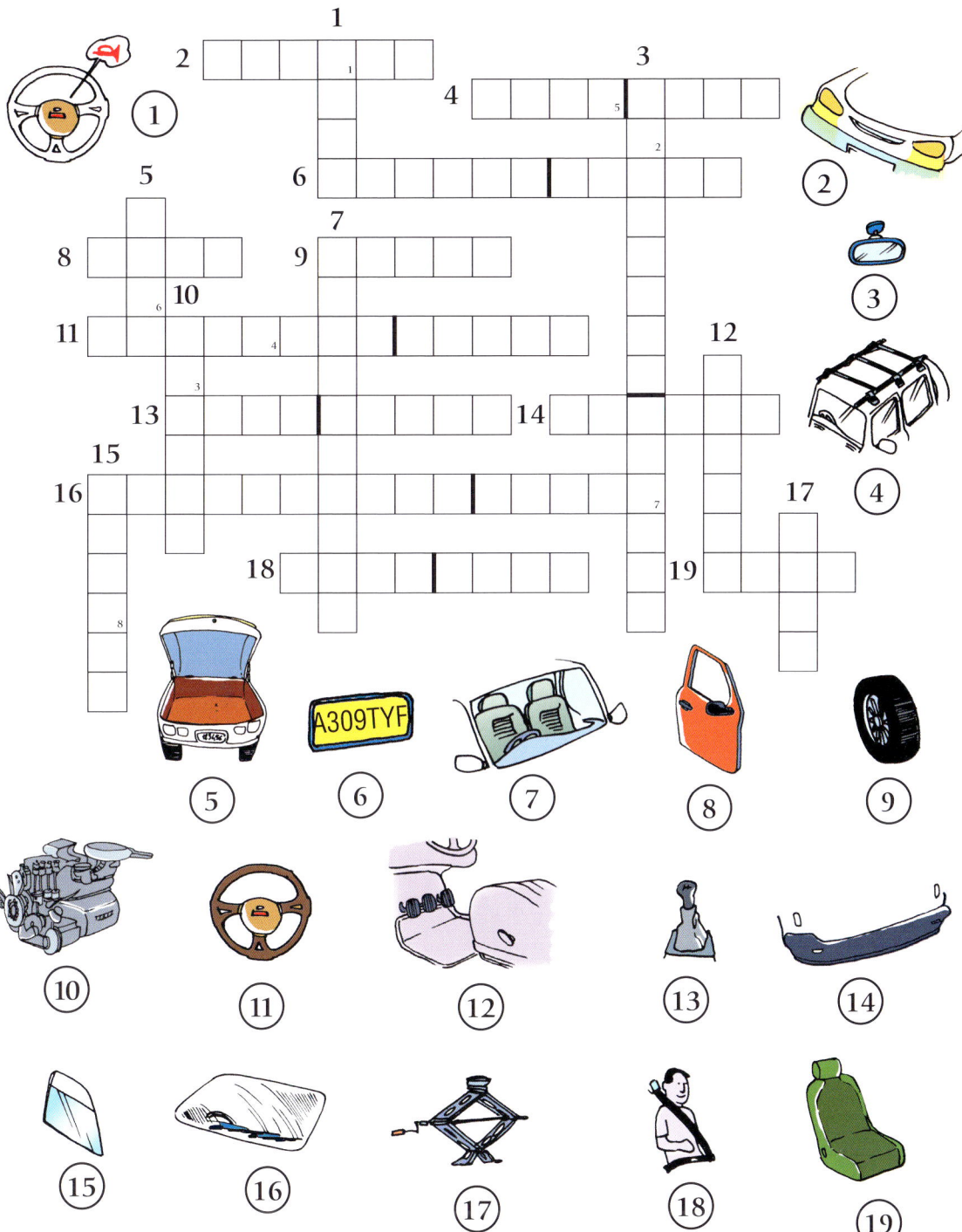

_ _ _ _ Y _ _ _ _ made the first motor car in 1896.
 1 2 3 4   5 6 7 8

Have you got a car?

Trains

1 Look and write the correct words.

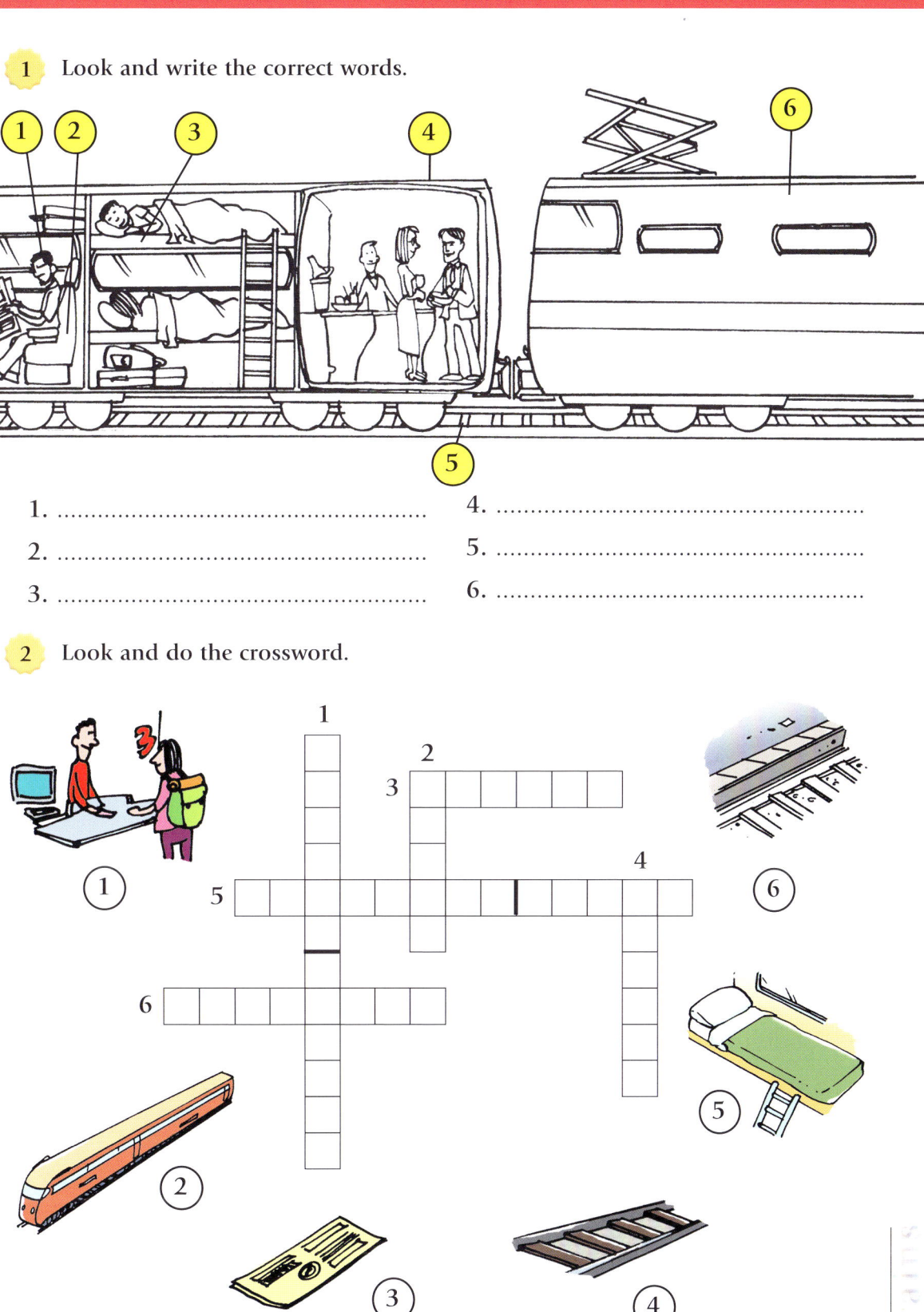

1. ....
2. ....
3. ....
4. ....
5. ....
6. ....

2 Look and do the crossword.

35

grammar

We use prepositions before nouns and pronouns.
Prepositions of movement describe direction.
This train is going **to** London.
That train is coming **from** London.
The train **to** London is leaving **from** platform 3.

Other prepositions of movement are **up**, **down**, **into**, **over**, **out of**, **across**, **along**, **towards**.

Prepositions of place describe where things happen.
She is **in** the waiting room.
He is **on** the platform.
They are **at** the timetable.
Other prepositions of place are **next to**, **near**, **in front of**, **behind**, **opposite**, **under**, **above**, **below**, **between**, **outside**, **inside**.

3 Complete the sentences with the best prepositions.

1. Where is this train going *in/to* ....?

2. There are lots of people *at/in* .... the waiting room.

3. Let's put our bags *in/on* .... the trolley.

4. Your train is leaving *from/on* .... platform 5.

5. There's a buffet service *at/on* .... this train.

6. You must put your ticket *in/on* .... the ticket gate before you get *in/on* .... the train.

7. She's standing *at/in* .... the window.

8. I put the tickets *at/in* .... my bag.

9. She left her bag *at/on* .... the sleeping berth.

10. She wants a seat *at/in* .... that carriage.

4 Look then choose a preposition and write the correct word.

1. Felix is getting *on/up* .... the ....

2. The train is arriving *at/in* .... 9.

3. Melanie is giving her ticket *at/to* .... the ....

4. Jim always leaves his bags *in/from* ....
....

5. These people are waiting *at/to* ....
the ....

6. Frank is sitting *at/on* .... his ....

7. Don't lean *out of/over* .... the ....

5 What is it?

1. You use it if your bags are heavy.
   It's a ....
2. You buy your tickets here.
   It's a ....
3. You read train times and platform numbers on this.
   It's a ....
4. You can sit here if you are early for your train.
   It's a ....
5. You can get one if you travel at night.
   It's a ....
6. You can leave your bags here.
   It's ....

6 At the station. Look and write.

1. .... 6. ....
2. .... 7. ....
3. .... 8. ....
4. .... 9. ....
5. .... 10. ....

7 Read and answer.

1. Angela usually buys a single ticket when she goes to London.
   What is a single ticket?
   ☐ **a.** A ticket for one passenger.
   ☐ **b.** A ticket for one train journey.

2. If you don't have a ticket the ticket collector will give you a fine.
   What is a fine?
   ☐ **a.** Money you pay as a punishment for something wrong.
   ☐ **b.** A ticket you can buy on the train.

8 Do the crossword.

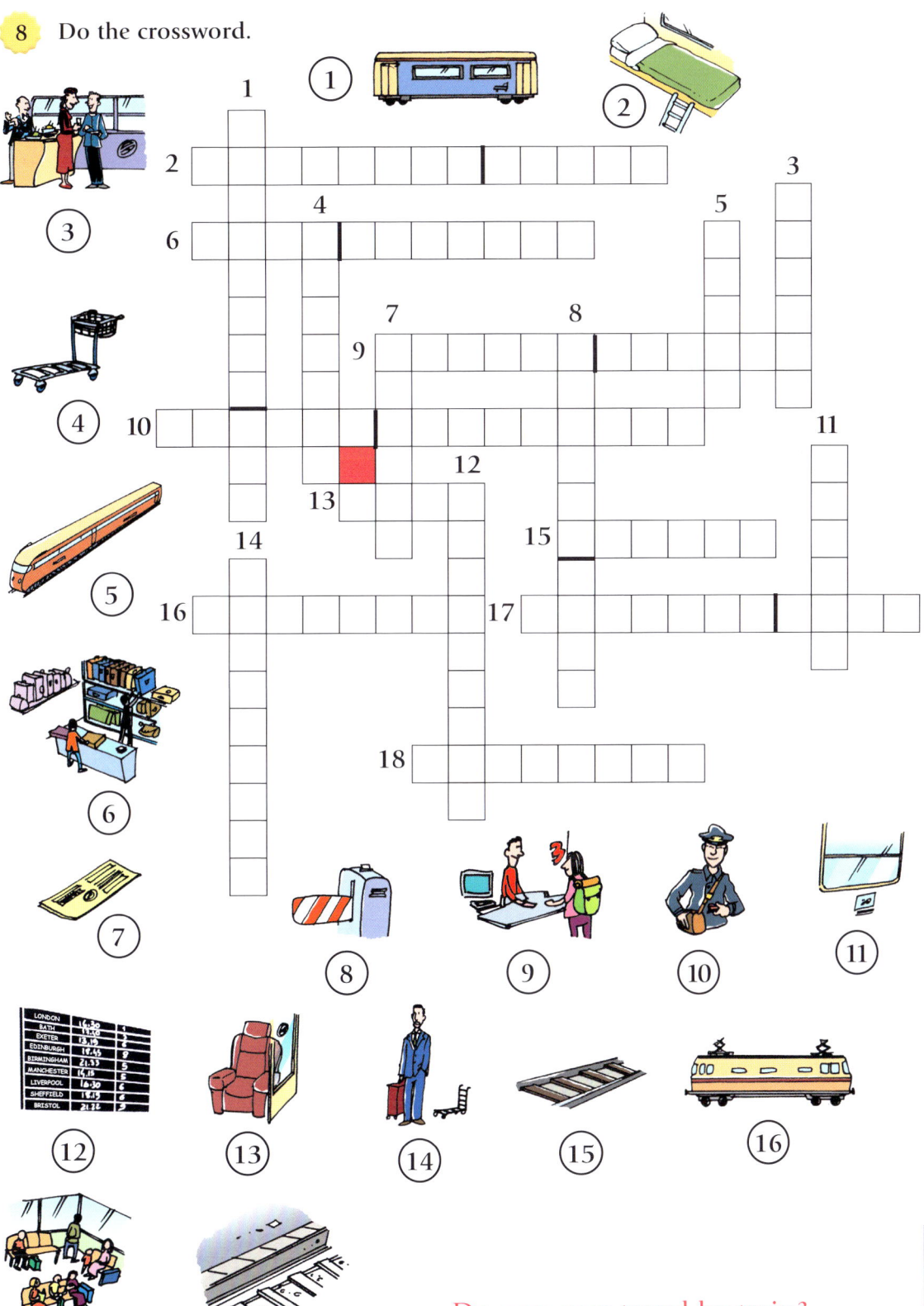

Do you ever travel by train?
Do you like it? Why/Why not?

Flying

 aeroplane
 control tower
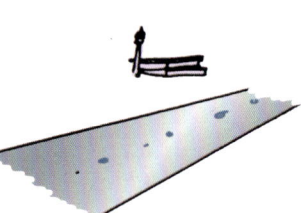 runway
 landing

 take-off
 check-in
 boarding card
 passport

 luggage
 metal detector
 gate
 pilot

 flight attendant
 seat
 seat belt
 window

 aisle
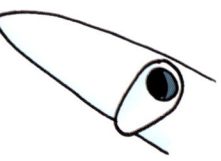 wing
 emergency exit
 baggage reclaim

1. Find eight words in the wordsearch box. The remaining letters spell the name of the very first aeroplane.

A	E	R	O	P	L	A	N	E	F	G
R	U	N	W	A	Y	W	I	N	G	A
L	U	G	G	A	G	E	L	Y	E	T
P	I	L	O	T	R	A	I	S	L	E
O	N	P	A	S	S	P	O	R	T	E

The name of the very first aeroplane is _ _ _ _ _ _ _ _.

2. Look at the drawing and write the correct words.

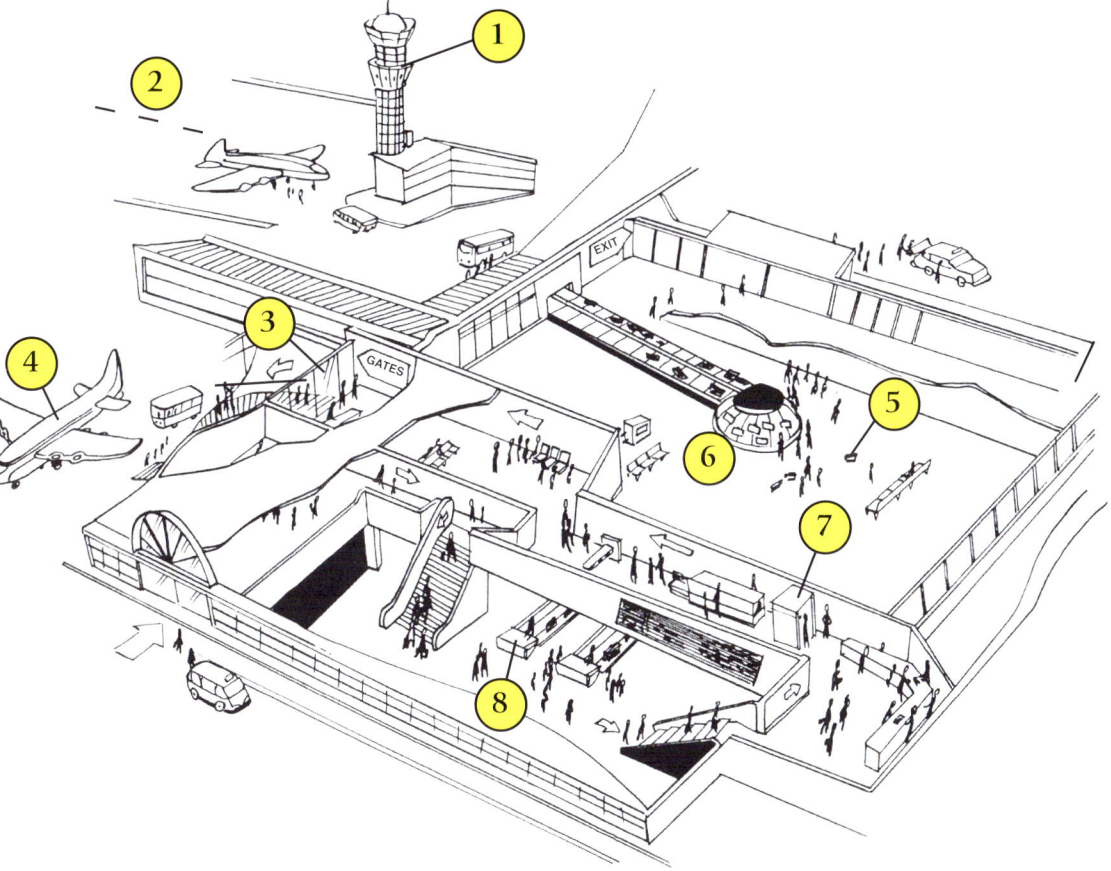

1. .... 5. ....
2. .... 6. ....
3. .... 7. ....
4. .... 8. ....

grammar

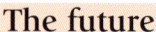

The future

We use the present simple when we talk about travel plans or timetables.
You **fly** to London at four o'clock tomorrow afternoon.

We use the present continuous or **be going to** *for future plans and intentions.*
We **aren't meeting** them at the check-in.
We **aren't going to** take much luggage with us.

We use **will be** *and* **won't be** *for future predictions.*
There **won't be** too many people at the baggage reclaim because it's very late.

We use **about to** *for actions in the very near future.*
The aeroplane **is about to** take off.

3 Look at the drawings and complete the sentences with the correct future tenses.

1. The aeroplane .... (to land).

2. The flight attendant .... (to apologize) to the passenger.

3. I .... (to fasten) my seat belt.

4. The porters .... (to load) the luggage onto the aeroplane.

5. After the pilot speaks to the passengers he .... (take off).

6. If Mark doesn't hurry up he .... (to miss) the bus.

4 Edward's flight to New York leaves soon. Complete the sentences then put them in the correct order.

a. ☐ He shows the airport policeman his ....

b. ☐ He goes to the ....

c. ☐ He gets a ....

d. ☐ Edward goes to the ....

e. ☐ He fastens his ....

f. ☐ And finally his .... takes off.

g. ☐ He goes through the ....

5 Who or what is it?

1. S/he looks after the passengers during the flight.
   NAGHTLITENFTADT   _ _ _ _ _ _   _ _ _ _ _ _ _ _
2. You need this to get on the aeroplane.
   DOBARDARCGIN   _ _ _ _ _ _ _ _   _ _ _ _
3. It makes a noise if you are carrying money, or a knife.
   DECTEAMELROTT   _ _ _ _ _   _ _ _ _ _ _ _ _
4. You get your luggage here after the flight.
   CLIGREAGAGEBAM   _ _ _ _ _ _ _   _ _ _ _ _ _ _

6 Look at the drawings and complete the sentences.

1. Have you got any ....?

2. Would you like a .... seat or an .... seat?

3. Here's your ....

4. May I see your ...., please?

5. All the passengers must fasten their ....

6. Place your bag under the .... in front of you.

7 Match the words to their definitions.

1. runway

2. landing

3. take-off

4. check-in

5. emergency exit

6. gate

a. It is the exit you use to go to your aeroplane.

b. It is where you go out of the aeroplane if there is a problem.

c. It is the 'road' where aeroplanes take off and land.

d. It is the time when an aeroplane leaves the ground.

e. It is where passengers leave their luggage and get their boarding cards.

f. It is the time when an aeroplane reaches the ground again.

8 Look and do the crossword.

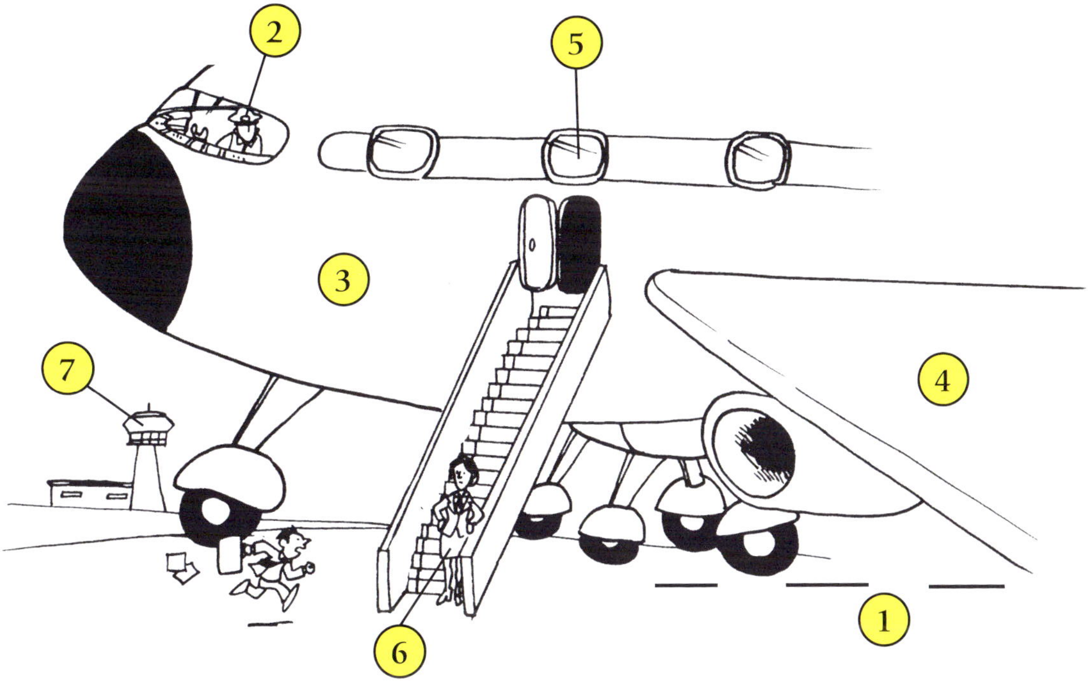

Do you like travelling by aeroplane?
Why/Why not?

Hotels

 half board

 full board

 reception

 lobby

 porter

 key

 single room

 double room

 twin room

 minibar

 air conditioning

 bar

 swimming pool

 car park

 restaurant

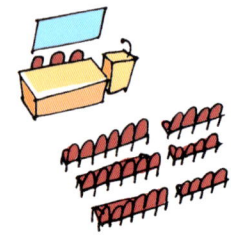 conference room

 gym

1 Look and write the correct words.

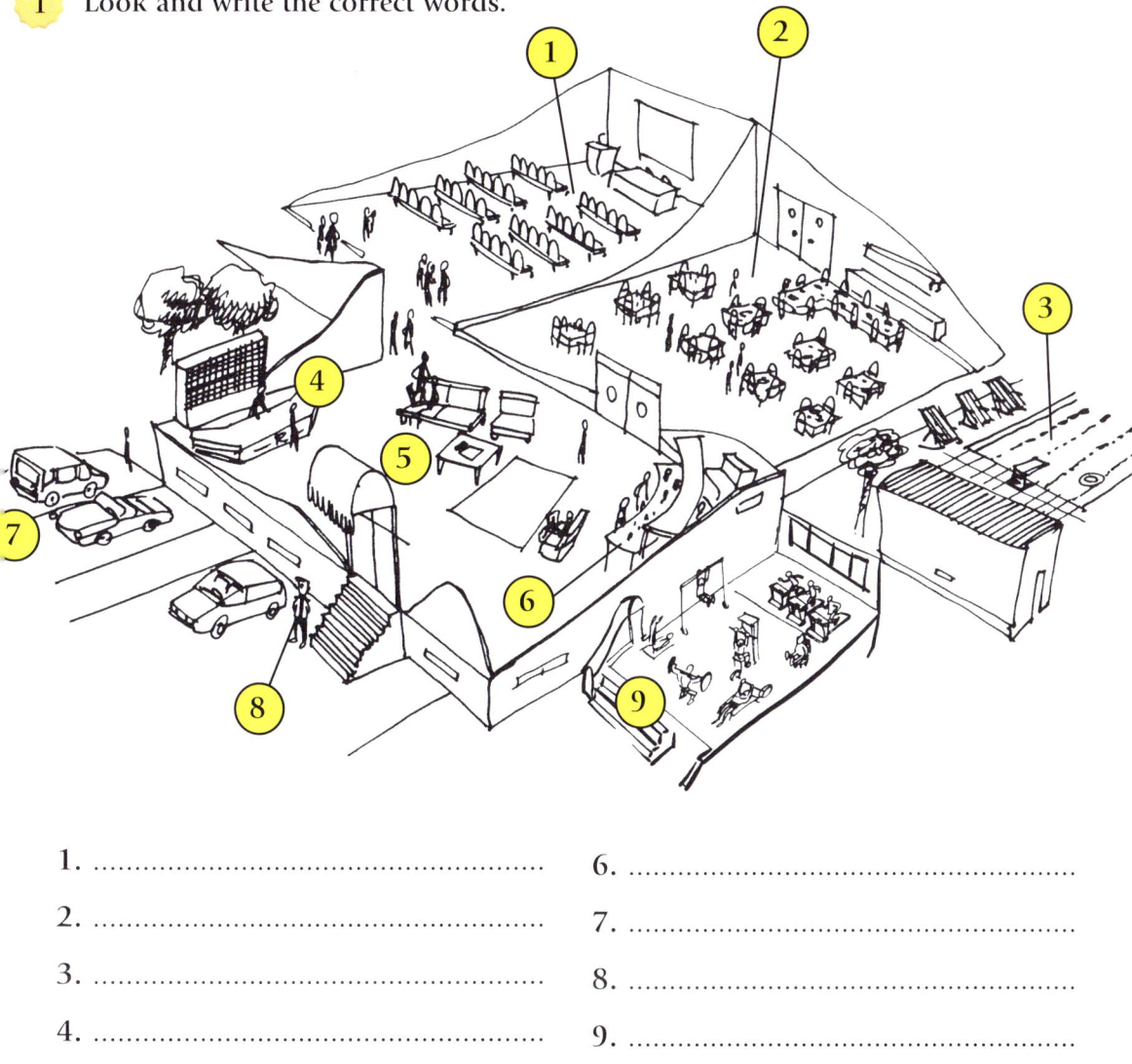

1. .... 6. ....
2. .... 7. ....
3. .... 8. ....
4. .... 9. ....
5. ....

2 What room? Read and decide what room they are going to book.

1. Mr Green is a business man. He's travelling on his own for work.

   He is going to book a ....

2. Shauna and Anne are sisters. They are on holiday together.

   They are going to book a ....

3. John and May-Ling are just married. They are on their honeymoon.

   They are going to book a ....

grammar

*We use **could** or **would** for making polite requests in English.*
Could I have a double room, please?
Would you like full board or half board?

*We use **could** or **may** to ask for permission. (We also use **can** but it is not as polite.)*
Could we change our room?
May I have room service, please?
Can I leave my bag at reception?

3 Complete these sentences with *could/would/may*.

1. .... I book a single room for one night, please?

2. .... it be possible to get a cot for our baby, please?

3. .... I smoke in my room?

4. .... we book in for dinner, too?

5. .... you like to see our gym?

6. .... we stay an extra night?

7. .... you sign this registration form, please?

8. .... you show me your passport, please?

4 Write four requests you could make in a hotel.

1. ....

2. ....

3. ....

4. ....

5 Rewrite the following sentences using polite forms.

1. I want a single room and full board.
   ....
2. Can I have a room with a view?
   ....?
3. I want a double room for next weekend.
   ....
4. I need air conditioning.
   ....?
5. Ask the porter.
   ....?
6. Go to reception.
   ....?
7. I want the key to room 132.
   ....
8. Is the conference room available?
   ....?

6 Do the crossword.

1. It's where you book in and get your room key.
2. It's a room with two single beds.
3. It's breakfast and either lunch or dinner.
4. It's where you eat.
5. It's the hall in a hotel where you can sit.
6. It's breakfast, lunch and dinner.

7 What has this hotel got?

1. The Highlow Hotel has 36 ....
2. There is a .... and .... in each room.
3. Both .... and .... are available.
4. The .... is open 24 hours a day.
5. There is a .... in the lobby where you can have a drink before going into the ....
6. There is a .... where you can relax.
7. There is also a large .... for your business meetings.
8. All clients can use the hotel ....

8 Unscramble the words.

1. You leave your car here.
   ARCKRAP _ _ _   _ _ _ _

2. You use it when it's very hot.
   ARIGINOCIDOTNIN _ _ _   _ _ _ _ _ _ _ _ _ _ _ _

3. You get one if you're travelling alone.
   GINSELMOOR _ _ _ _ _ _   _ _ _ _

4. It's useful if you get thirsty at night.
   NAMIBIR _ _ _ _ _ _ _

5. You can have meetings here.
   CEFENORCENMOOR _ _ _ _ _ _ _ _ _ _   _ _ _ _

6. S/he helps you with your bags.
   TERROP _ _ _ _ _ _

9 Find the words from this unit in the wordsearch box. The remaining letters spell the name of a famous hotel and a famous book.

A	I	R	C	O	N	D	I	T	I	O	N	I	N	G
D	O	U	B	L	E	R	O	O	M	T	H	G	Y	M
E	C	O	N	F	E	R	E	N	C	E	R	O	O	M
L	O	B	B	Y	O	H	A	L	F	B	O	A	R	D
B	A	R	R	R	E	C	E	P	T	I	O	N	M	K
O	P	O	R	T	E	R	C	A	R	P	A	R	K	E
N	D	R	E	S	T	A	U	R	A	N	T	Q	U	Y
M	I	N	I	B	A	R	T	W	I	N	R	O	O	M
A	Y	S	I	N	G	L	E	R	O	O	M	H	O	T
E	S	W	I	M	M	I	N	G	P	O	O	L	L	U
L	Y	S	F	U	L	L	B	O	A	R	D	S	E	S

In _ _ _   _ _ _ _ _ _ _   _ _ _ _   _ _ _ _ _ in Dublin,
James Joyce wrote some of his masterpiece _ _ _ _ _ _ _.

What do you like about hotels?
What do you dislike?

Music

1. Look and do the crossword.

2. Find nine words in the wordsearch box. Use the remaining letters to complete the sentence.

```
S  A  X  O  P  H  O  N  E  P
K  E  Y  B  O  A  R  D  D  I
V  I  O  L  I  N  I  N  R  A
S  F  L  U  T  E  T  R  U  N
U  M  C  E  L  L  O  E  M  O
N  T  R  U  M  P  E  T  S  T
A  C  C  O  R  D  I  O  N  S
```

They are all musical _ _ _ _ _ _ _ _ _ _ _ .

53

grammar

Past simple

I played
You played
He played
She played
It played
We played
You played
They played

*In English we use the **past simple** for actions that started and finished in the past.*
*We add **-ed** or **-d** to the verb in order to make the past simple.*

Sally **played** the piano at school.
Ted **liked** playing the guitar.

We double the consonant after 1-syllable verbs ending in a vowel + consonant.
When the music **stopped** everyone **clapped**.

*We change **y** to **-ied**.*
He **tried** to play the piano.

3 Look at the drawings, write the past simple of *play* and the correct word.

1. David .... the _ _ _ _ _.

3. They .... the _ _ _ _ _ _.

2. Mr and Mrs Murphy .... in a _ _ _ _.

4. Theo .... the _ _ _ _ _ very well.

4 Look and write the words.

1. ....
2. ....
3. ....
4. ....
5. ....
6. ....

5 Complete the sentences with the correct words.

1. John really liked the  ....

2. The  .... played at the festival.

3. I listened to U2's latest  ....

4. George wanted to be a  ....

5. Sid played in a  ....

6. I tried to play the  .... at school.

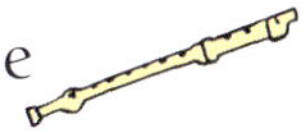

6 Do you know your music? Match the following pieces of music with the correct musical genres.

folk – opera – rock – classical – jazz – blues – rap – pop

1. *Spring,* Vivaldi
   ....
2. *Madame Butterfly,* Puccini
   ....
3. *Sunday, Bloody Sunday,* U2
   ....
4. *Yesterday,* The Beatles
   ....
5. *Cornet Chop Suey,* Louis Armstrong
   ....
6. *Strange Fruit,* Nina Simone
   ....
7. *8 mile,* Eminem
   ....
8. *Hard Rain,* Bob Dylan
   ....

7 Which instruments do you most associate with the following musical genres?

1. classical
2. folk
3. blues
4. rock
5. jazz

a. saxophone, trumpet, double-bass
b. keyboard, drums, guitar
c. guitar
d. violin, piano, flute, cello
e. guitar, trumpet

8 Do the crossword.

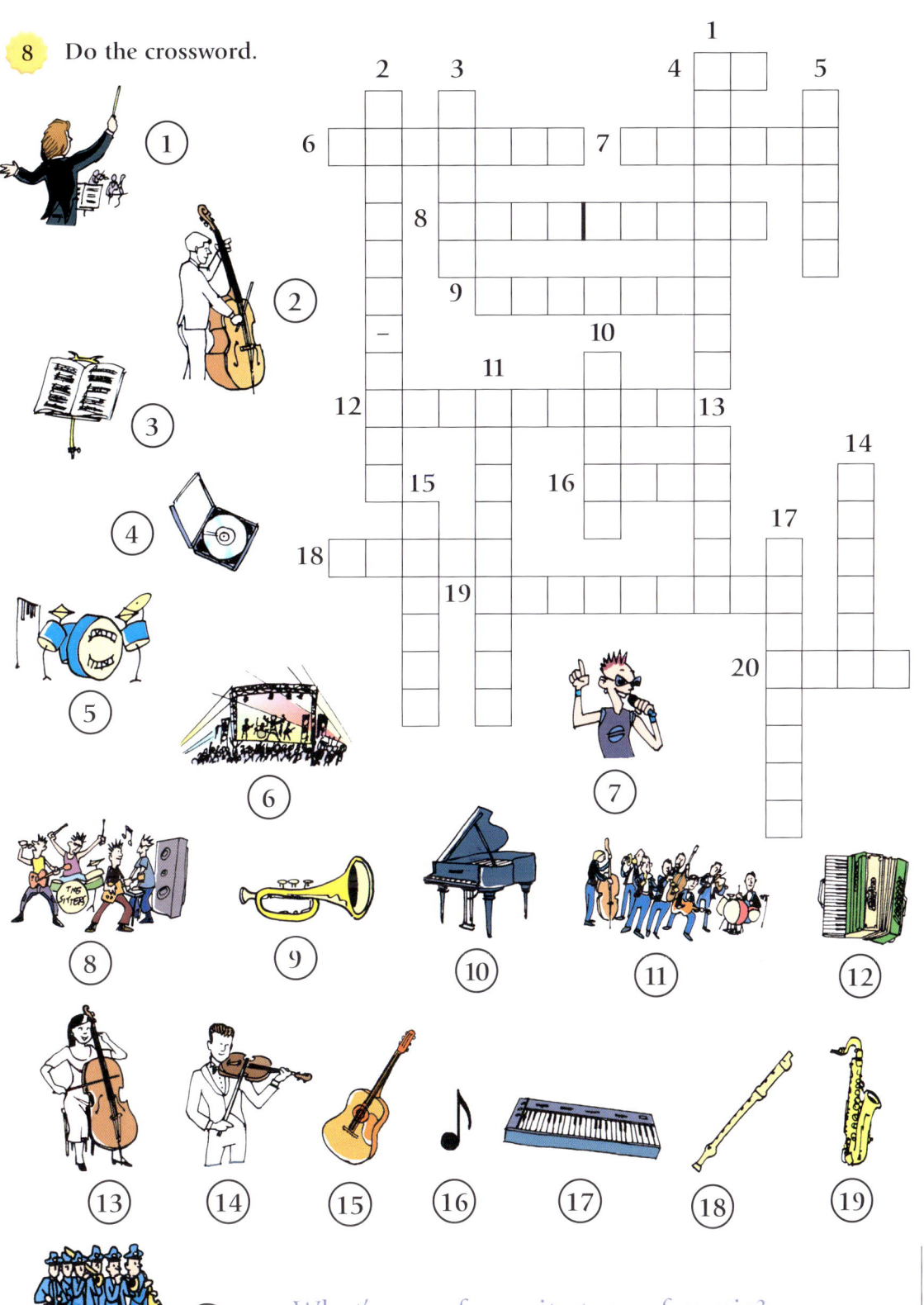

What's your favourite type of music?
Can you play an instrument?

Films and plays

box office

ticket

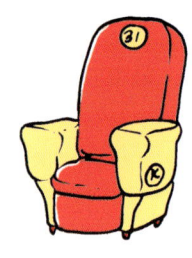
seat

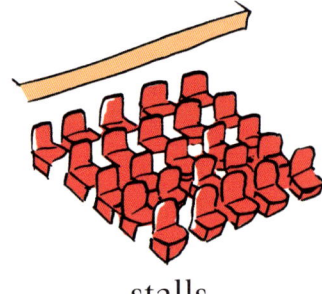
stalls

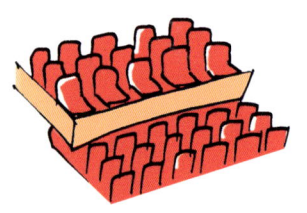
gallery

screen

director

film

poster

box

stage

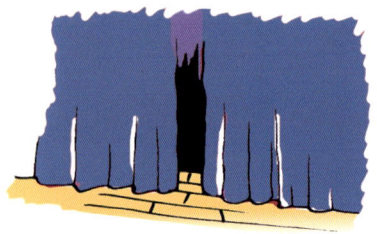
curtain

actor

actress

1 Write the words in the grid. Use the letters in the grey boxes to complete the name of a famous play by Shakespeare.

H _ _ _ _ _ is a famous play by Shakespeare.

2 Do the crossword. Use the letters in the grey boxes to spell the name of a famous film.

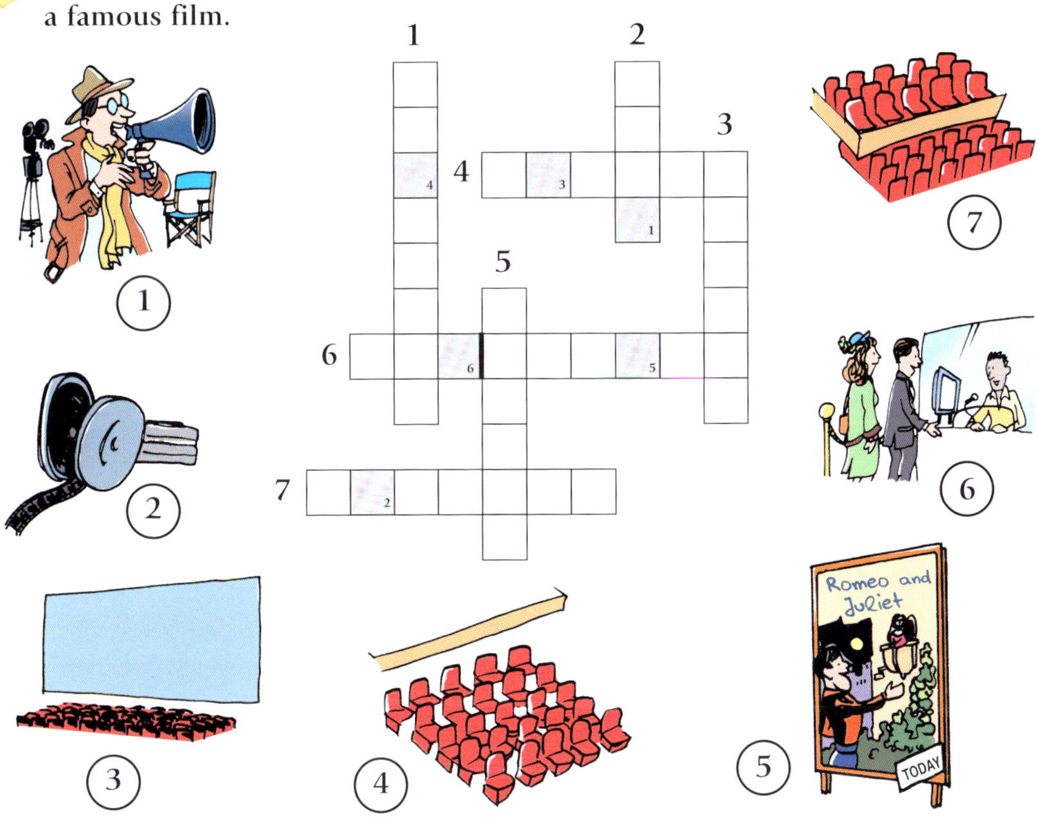

_ _ _ _ _ _ is a famous science-fiction trilogy.
 1 2 3 4 5 6

grammar

Past simple

Negative	Interrogative
I didn't play	Did I play?
You didn't play	Did you play?
He didn't play	Did he play?
She didn't play	Did she play?
It didn't play	Did it play?
We didn't play	Did we play?
You didn't play	Did you play?
They didn't play	Did they play?

We can make short answers.
Did you like the film?
Yes, I did. / No, I didn't.

3 Write short answers to the following questions.

1. Did she like the play? Yes, ………………………… .

2. Did the director like the actors? No, ………………………… .

3. Did you like the film? No, ………………………… .

4. Did the people like the actress? Yes, ………………………… .

5. Did they like the film? No, ………………………… .

4 Look at the drawings and write the questions.

Did you sit far from the screen?

2. .... (you sit) in front of the _ _ _ _ _ _ _?

1. .... (they sit) in the _ _ _ _ _ _ _?

3. .... (he sit) in the _ _ _ _ _ _?

5 What is it?

1. You get your ticket here.
   ....

2. The actors and actresses stand here.
   ....

3. It shows what film or play is on.
   ....

4. It opens and closes at the beginning and end of a play.
   ....

5. It's where you look in a cinema.
   ....

6. It's like a small balcony in a theatre where you can watch the play.
   ....

6 Read the definitions and find the words in the wordsearch box.
The remaining letters spell out a phrase that actors say to mean 'Good luck!'.

B R T I C K E T E
A K A P O S T E R
D I R E C T O R L
E G A L L E R Y G

Actors say "_ _ _ _ _ _ _ _ _"
before they go on stage.

1. It's upstairs in a cinema or theatre. ....
2. You read it to see what film or play you want to see. ....
3. You need it to go into a cinema or theatre. ....
4. He or she tells the actors what to do. ....

7 Look and write the correct words.

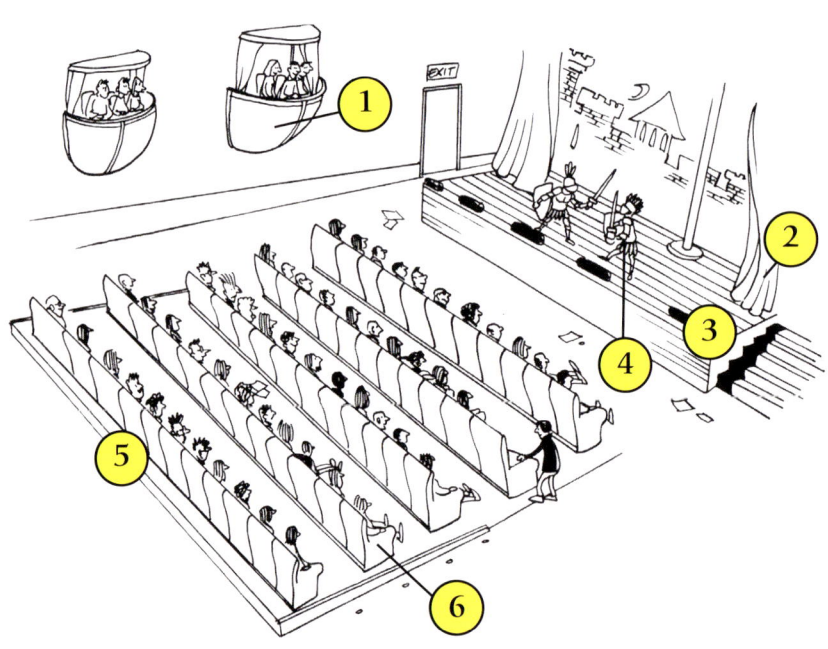

1. ....
2. ....
3. ....
4. ....
5. ....
6. ....

8 Do the crossword.

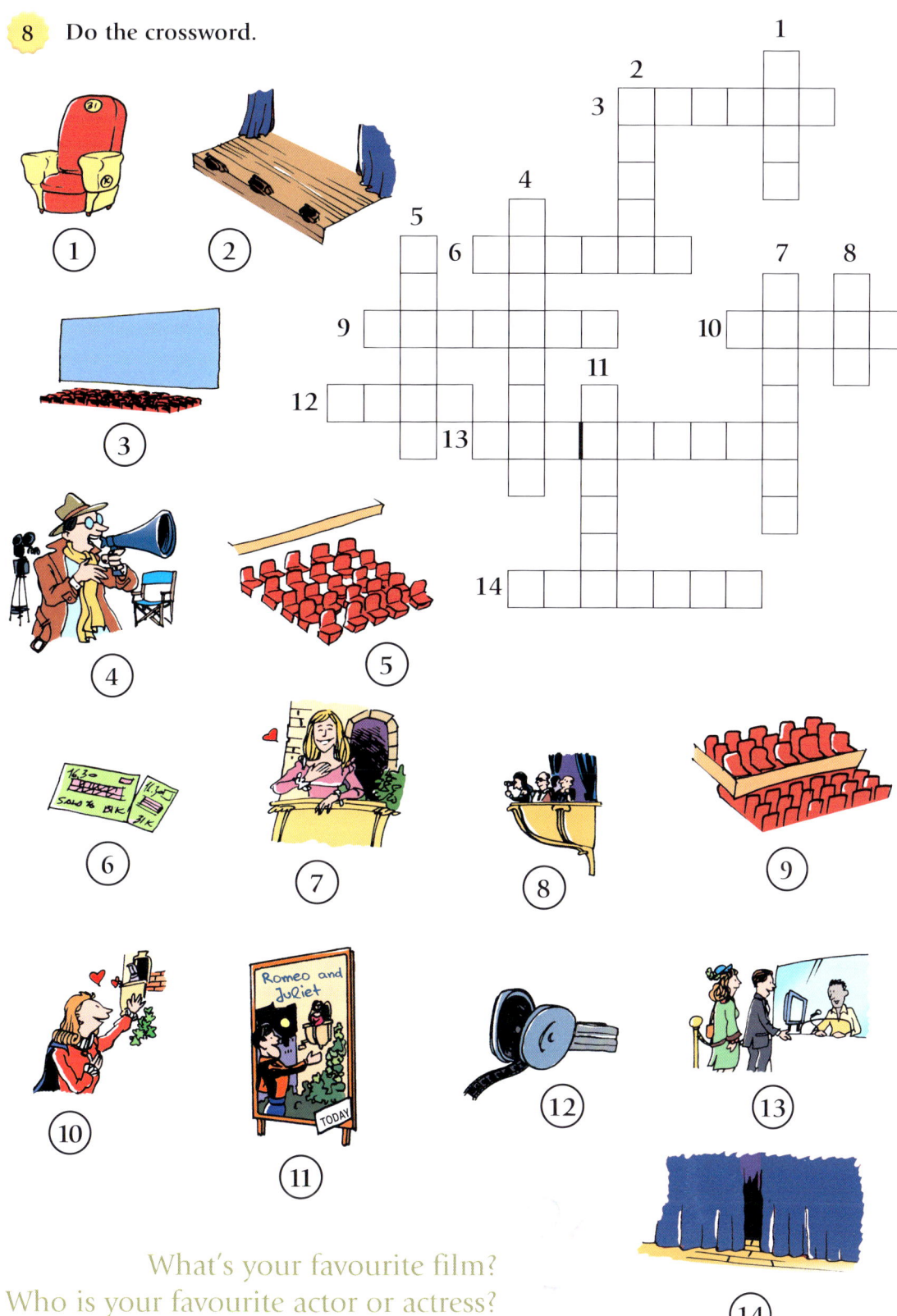

What's your favourite film?
Who is your favourite actor or actress?

Television

television set   remote control   DVD player   video recorder

  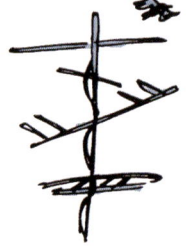 

videotape   TV guide   aerial   news

talk show   game show   film   documentary

cartoon   commercial   weather forecast   sports programme

1. Look at the drawings and do the crossword. Then use the letters in the grey boxes to complete the sentence below.

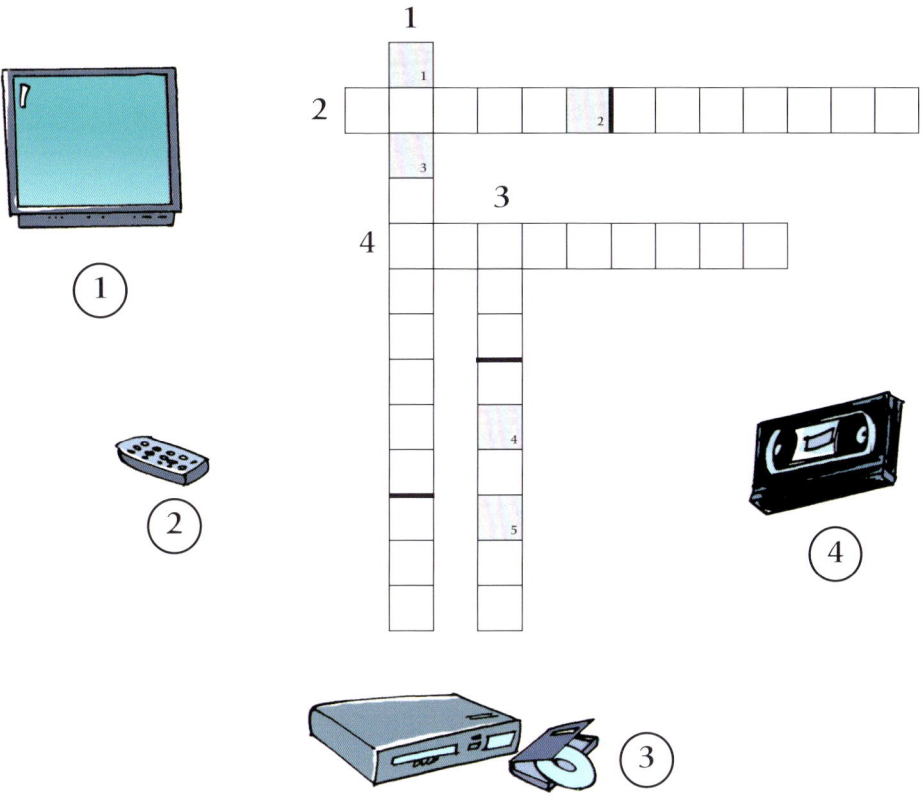

_ _ _ _ _ is a popular word for television.
  1 2 3 4 5

2. Find six words in the wordsearch box. Then use the remaining letters to complete the sentence.

D	O	C	U	M	E	N	T	A	R	Y
N	S	C	A	R	T	O	O	N	O	A
E	G	A	M	E	S	H	O	W	P	O
W	P	E	T	A	L	K	S	H	O	W
S	R	A	S	F	I	L	M	A	R	E

_ _ _ _   _ _ _ _ _ _ _   _ _ _ television programmes with lots of episodes.

grammar

*In the past simple irregular verbs have a special form in the affirmative. The negative and interrogative is formed with **did not** and **Did ...?***

I saw a film last night.
Did you see the news yesterday?
I didn't see the documentary on Saturday.

Here are some commonly used irregular past simples.

begin	began
break	broke
buy	bought
come	came
do	did
get	got
give	gave
have	had
know	knew
make	made
read	read
see	saw
take	took
think	thought
win	won

3 Look at the drawings then complete the sentences with the correct words and verb

1. She .... (read) the _ _ _ _ _ _ _ yesterday.

2. They .... (see) the _ _ _ _ yesterday.

3. I .... (give) him my _ _ _ _ _ _ _ _ _.

4. We .... (buy) a new _ _ _ _ _ _ _ _ _ _ _ _ _.

5. I .... (think) that _ _ _ _ _ _ _ _ _ _ was very good.

6. You .... (have) lots of _ _ _ _ _ _ _ _ _.

4 Match the programmes to the descriptions.

1. ☐ news
2. ☐ talk show
3. ☐ game show
4. ☐ film
5. ☐ documentary
6. ☐ cartoon
7. ☐ weather forecast
8. ☐ sports programme

a. Rain, sun or snow
b. Football crazy
c. A story of love and revenge
d. News from around the world
e. Donald, Mickey and friends
f. And the winner is …
g. Our special guest is …
h. A day in the jungle

5 What is it?

1. You use it to turn the TV on and off.
   ....

2. You use it to watch videotapes.
   ....

3. You use it to decide what programmes you want to watch.
   ....

4. You need one in order to be able to see television channels.
   ....

6 What did they watch? Read and decide what programmes they watched.

1. Miriam wanted to find out what happened that day.
   So she watched the ....

2. John saw the football results on the ....

3. Charlie wanted to check the weather so he watched the
   ....

4. My children always watched ....
   like Popeye before they went to bed.

5. Dan was interested in wildlife.
   He liked watching ....

6. Monica always watched .... on the TV
   if she didn't see them at the cinema.

7. Paul loved testing his general knowledge by watching
   ....

8. Janet loved gossip and news about the stars so she never missed
   a ....

9. Sid worked for an advertising agency so he liked watching
   ....

7 Do the crossword.

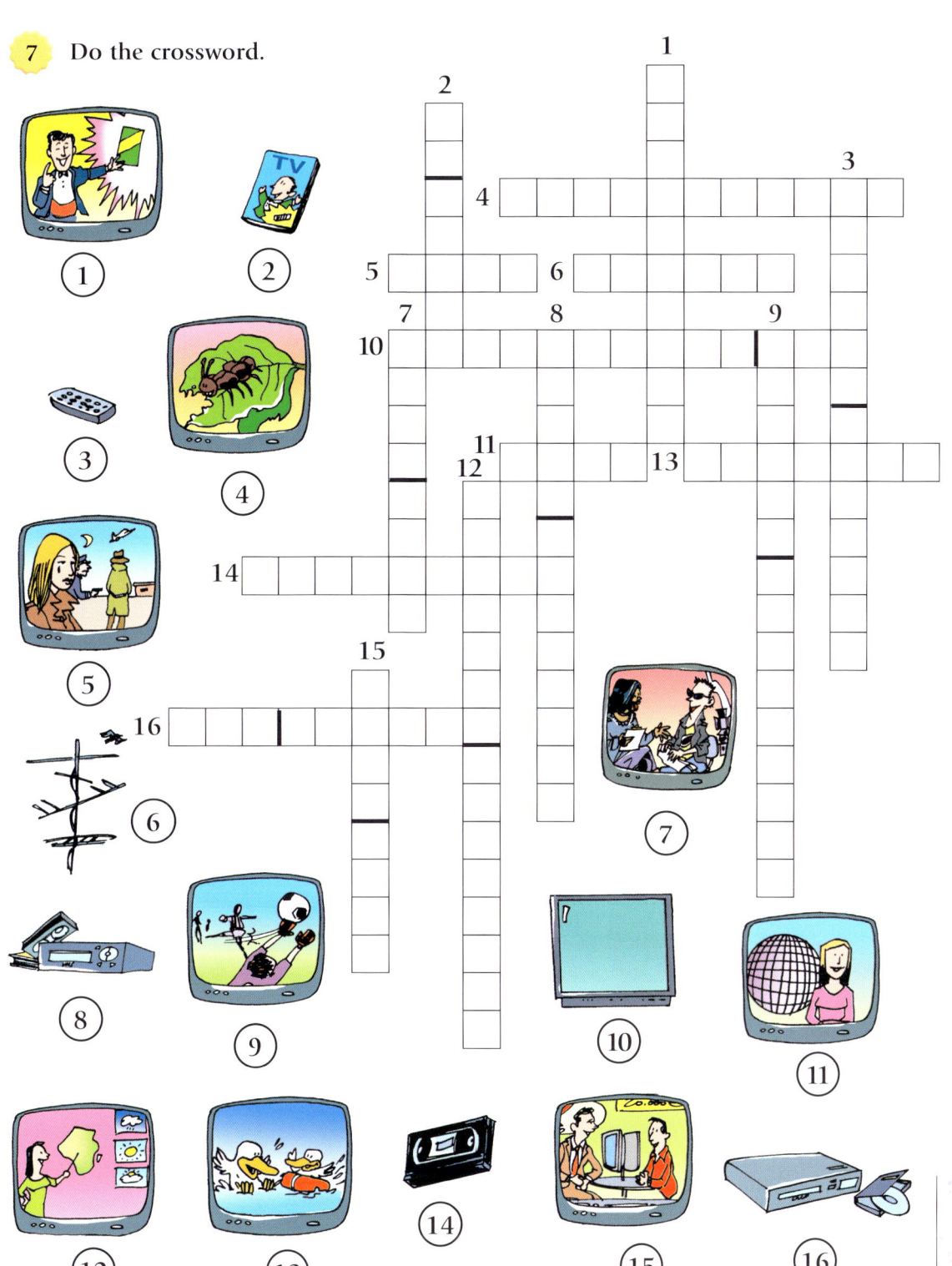

Do you watch much TV?
What are your favourite programmes?

Technology

 camcorder

 camera

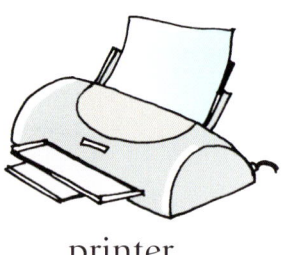 computer

printer

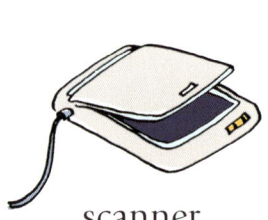 scanner

 laptop

 photocopier

 fax

 calculator

 radio

Walkman

 CD player/ Discman

 hi-fi

 car radio

 telephone

 mobile phone

 answering machine

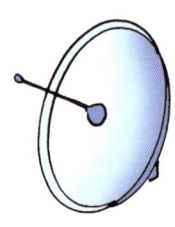 satellite dish

1 Write the words under the correct headings.

camcorder – car radio – calculator – hi-fi – mobile phone
CD player – Walkman – fax – telephone – radio

Music	Communications	Other
....	....	....
....	....	....
....	....	....
....	....	....
....	....	....

2 Look at the drawing and write numbers.

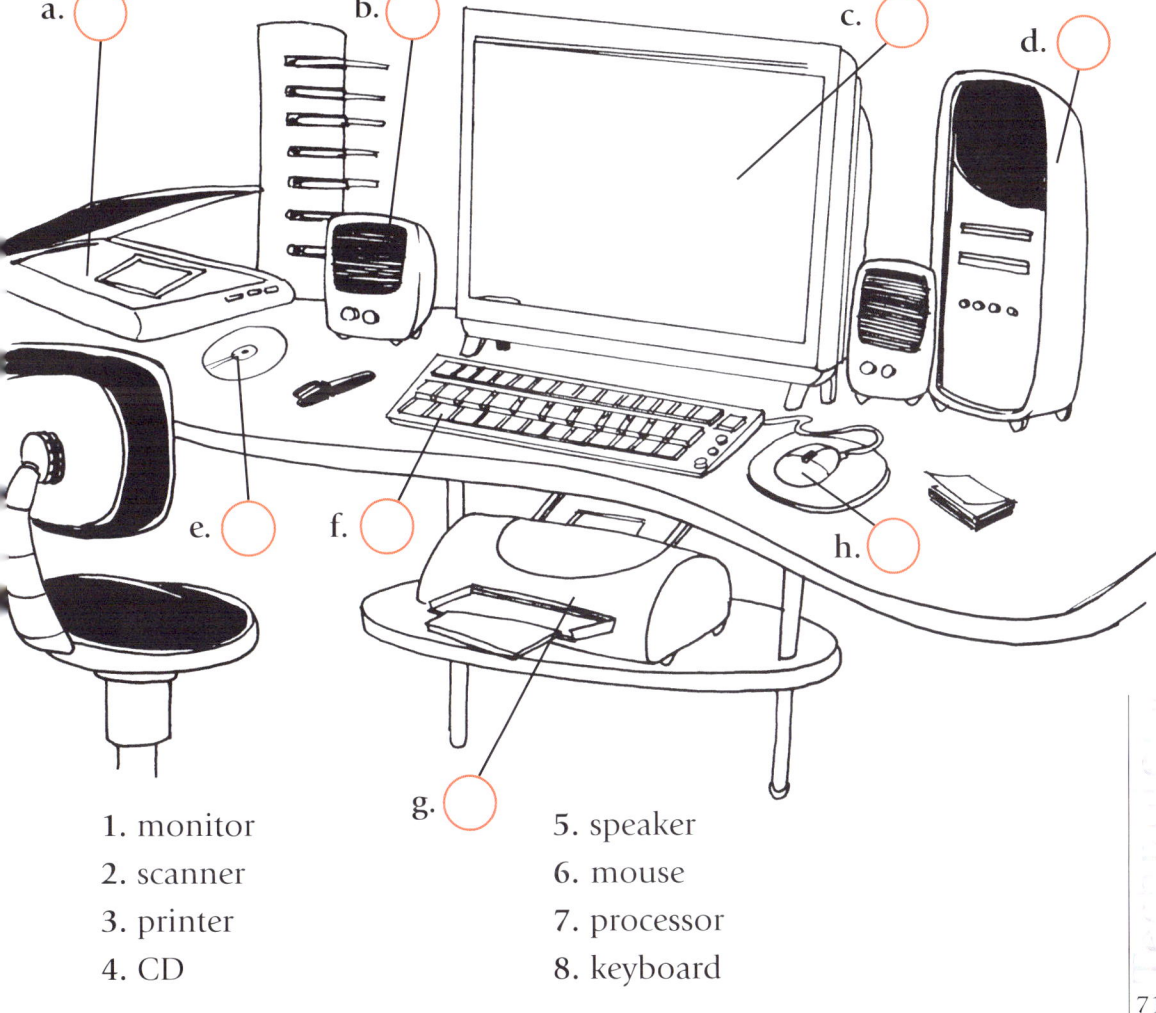

1. monitor
2. scanner
3. printer
4. CD
5. speaker
6. mouse
7. processor
8. keyboard

grammar

Past simple of 'be'

I was	I was not (wasn't)	Was I?
You were	You were not (weren't)	Were you?
He was	He was not (wasn't)	Was he?
She was	She was not (wasn't)	Was she?
It was	It was not (wasn't)	Was it?
We were	We were not (weren't)	Were we?
You were	You were not (weren't)	Were you?
They were	They were not (weren't)	Were they?

Was the fax on the table?
Yes, it **was**. / No, it **wasn't**.

3 Then and now. Complete with the correct word and the past of *be*.

1. In the past there .... lots of public phones.

    Now most people have a  _ _ _ _ _ _   _ _ _ _ _.

2. Twenty years ago there .... a typewriter on that desk.

    Now there is a 🖥️ _ _ _ _ _ _ _ _.

3. Letters .... popular in the past.

    Now people also use the 📠 _ _ _ to send urgent documents.

4. It .... difficult to make copies of documents in the past.

    Now we can use a 🖨️ _ _ _ _ _ _ _ _ _ _ _.

5. It .... trendy to have a  _ _ _ _ _ _ _ ten years ago.

    Now it is more trendy to have a  _ _   _ _ _ _ _ _.

4 Read then complete with the missing word.

1. Most cars have a  ....

2. I use my  .... more than my ....

3. I never write letters. I send emails on my 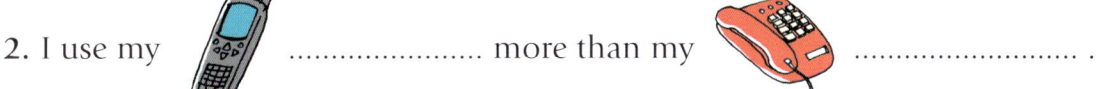 ....

4. I bought a new digital  ....

5 What do you need?

1. To listen to music?
2. To listen to a CD?
3. To add up a bill?
4. To find out who phoned?
5. To put a photo into your computer?
6. To listen to music in your car?
7. To get lots of foreign or pay TV channels?

6 Match the verbs and the objects.

1. to film
2. to take photographs
3. to print
4. to scan
5. to photocopy
6. to fax
7. to text

a. photocopier
b. scanner
c. fax
d. mobile phone
e. camcorder
f. printer
g. camera

7 Now put the verbs above in the past simple.

1. I .... everything I saw on holidays with my camcorder.

2. She .... her homework on the printer.

3. They .... us the documents from their fax.

4. We .... with our new digital camera.

5. You .... all your photos on your scanner.

6. I .... them on my mobile phone as soon as I arrived.

7. He .... a chapter of the book with the photocopier in work.

8 Where do you use them? Write where you use the things in this unit.

At home/at work	....
	....
	....
	....
In the car	....
Elsewhere	....
	....
	....

9 Do the crossword.

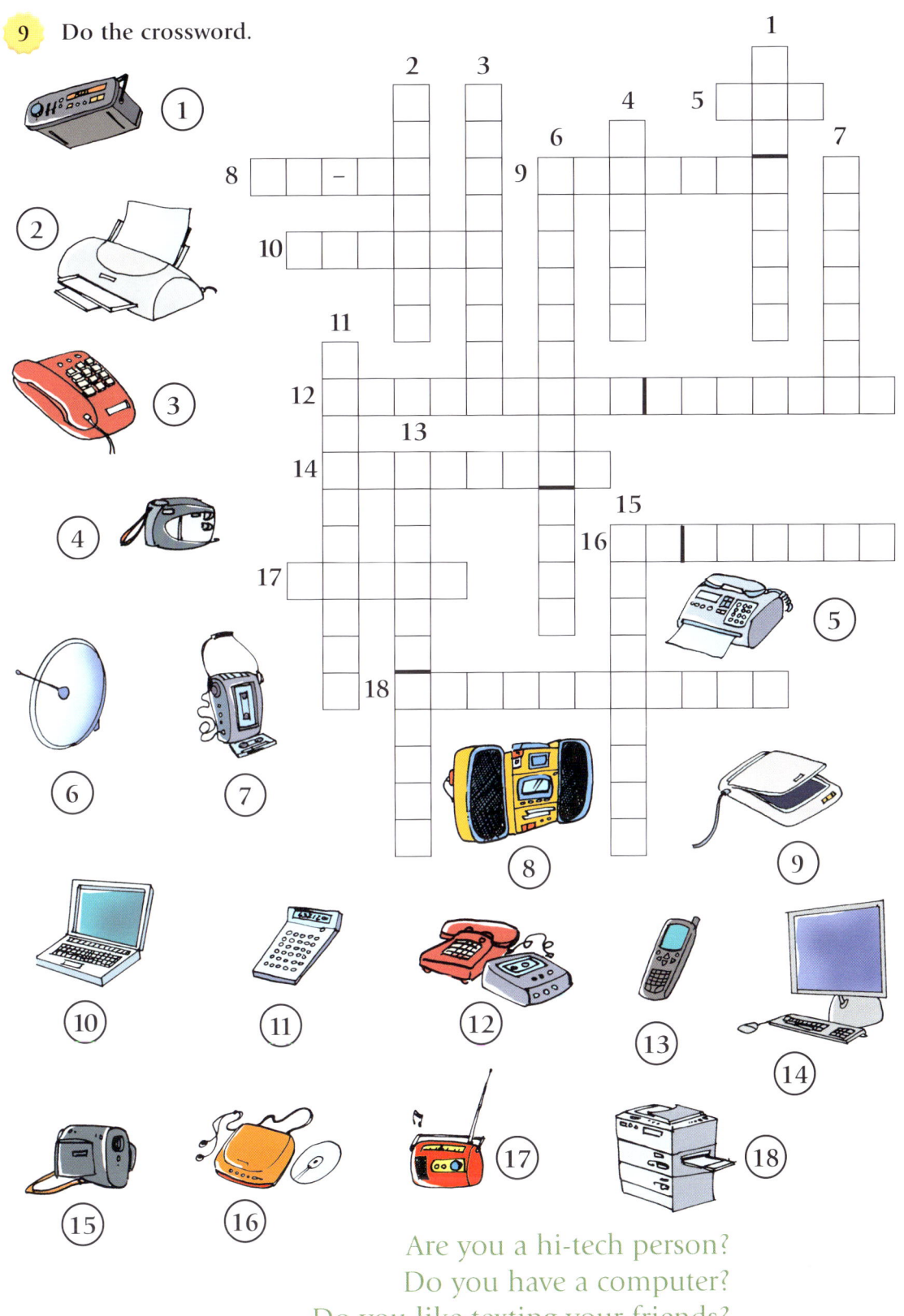

Are you a hi-tech person?
Do you have a computer?
Do you like texting your friends?

Sport II

 high jump

 long jump

 hurdles

 weightlifting

 squash

 karate

 American football

 windsurfing

 skateboarding

 ice hockey

 baseball

 diving

 motorcycling

 table tennis

 boxing

 rowing

 bobsleighing

1 Look and write the sports. Use the letters in the grey boxes to complete the sentence below.

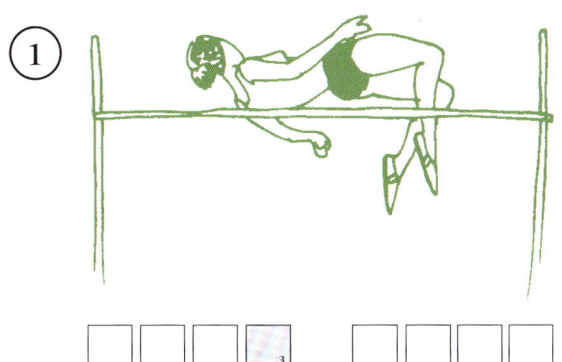

These three sports are all part of the _ _ CAT _ _ _ _.
                                      1 2   3 4 5 6

How many events are there in this sport? ....

2 Match the sport with the equipment.

1. boxing   a. oar
2. table tennis   b. knee pads
3. motorcycling   c. sail
4. windsurfing   d. ball
5. rowing   e. helmet
6. American football   f. gloves
7. skateboarding   g. bat, ball and net

77

grammar

Present perfect

You form the present perfect with the present simple of the verb 'have' plus the past participle of the verb. The past participle of regular verbs is the same as the past simple.

I have (I've) played
You have (you've) played
He has (he's) played
She has (she's) played
It has (it's) played
We have (we've) played
You have (you've) played
They have (they've) played

I have not (haven't) played
You have not (haven't) played
He has not (hasn't) played
She has not (hasn't) played
It has not (hasn't) played
We have not (haven't) played
You have not (haven't) played
They have not (haven't) played

We use the present perfect in the following cases.

1. For a past action that has an effect on the present.
Have they finished playing table tennis? I want to talk to them.
2. For a past action at an unknown or unsaid time.
Have you played American football?
3. With ever, never, just, already, yet.
She has never tried rowing.

3 Complete the following answers and questions.

1. Have they ever played squash?
   Yes, ...
2. Has he ever watched American football?
   No, ...
3. .... (you ever try) skateboarding?
   No, I've never tried skateboarding.
4. .... (you ever play) table tennis?
   Yes, we've played table tennis lots of times.

4 Find four sports in the wordsearch box. Use the remaining letters to complete the sentence.

A M E R I C A N F O O T B A L L R
E B A S E B A L L T E R O W I N G
A M I C E H O C K E Y S P O R T S

They'_ _ all _ _ _ _ _ _ _ _ _ _.

5 Write the names in the grid. Use the letters in the grey boxes to complete the sentence.

They are all _ _ _ _ _ _ _ _ _ _ sports.

6 And the winner is … What types of sports are these? Decide and write.

windsurfing – skateboarding – weightlifting – diving – bobsleighing
squash – rowing – hurdles – karate – American football – ice hockey
boxing – table tennis – baseball

Races	Games	Performance-based	Tests of strength

7 Here are some track and field sports. Write the three names you know.

a. 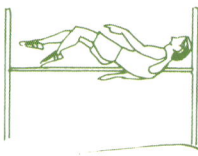 b.  c.

□□□□   □□□□   □□□□□□□
□□□□   □□□□

1. relay   2. sprint   3. steeplechase   4. walking

5. pole vault   6. triple jump   7. discus

8. javelin   9. shot-put   10. hammer

8 Do the crossword.

What sports have you tried?
What sports are popular in your country?

Daily actions

1 Match the verbs with the things.

1. ☐ pay
2. ☐ phone
3. ☐ go down
4. ☐ go up
5. ☐ turn on
6. ☐ clean
7. ☐ write
8. ☐ send
9. ☐ wait for

a. an email 
b. a bus 
c. the stairs 
d. a friend 
e. a poem 
f. a bill 
g. the ladder 
h. the floor 
i. the light

2 Look at the drawings and write the words in the grid. Use the letters in the grey boxes to complete the sentence below.

Things you do every day are part of your R _ _ _ _ _ _.
                             1 2 3 4 5 6

Daily actions

grammar

Many verbs are irregular in the present perfect.

be	been
find	found
go	gone
have	had
pay	paid
put	put
write	written
send	sent
take	taken

She's **gone** up to the attic.   They've **taken** the post.

Many verbs in English are followed by adverbs. The adverbs change the meaning of the base verb. Sometimes the meaning is clear (go in) *but sometimes it is difficult to understand* (cut down = use less). *These verbs are called* **phrasal verbs** *(see page 30).*

Go +   Go up   Go down
       Go in   Go out

3 Look and write using the present perfect or the past simple.

1. I think she .... (send) the letters.

2. I .... (wait for) John outside school yesterday.

3. He .... (turn on) the light when it was dark.

4. He .... (not finish) cleaning the car.

4 Match the opposite actions.

turn on – find – go up – go in

1. look for .... 3. go out ....

2. go down .... 4. turn off ....

5 Underline the correct tense.

1. When Luke *has gone in/went in* he *has turned on/turned on* the light.

2. I'm sorry *I haven't written/didn't write* for a long time.

3. *Have you paid/Did you pay* all your bills?

4. She *has put on/put on* her make-up before she *has gone out/went out*.

5. They *have waved/waved* when they *have gone into/went into* the bus.

6. I *have never written/never wrote* a poem.

6 Write sentences. How many combinations can you find with these verbs and adverbs? Use your dictionary to help you!

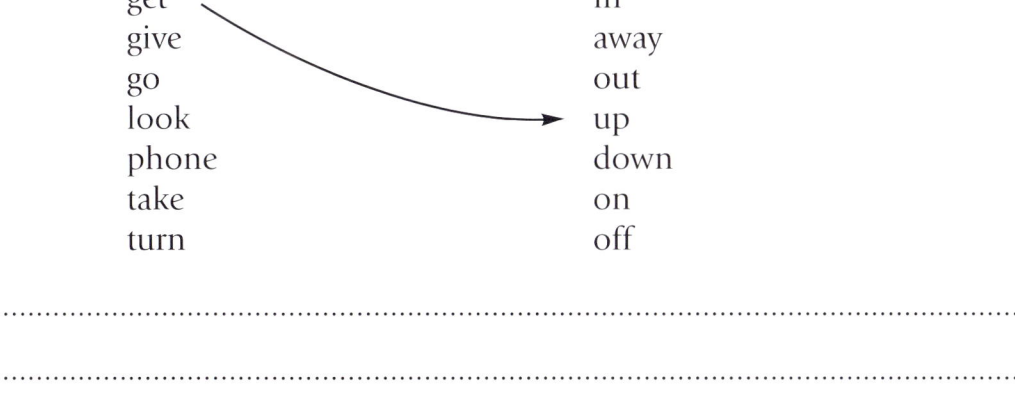

....

....

....

....

....

....

7 Dear Delia ... Complete Jack's letter to Delia with the correct past tense.

Dear Delia,
I'm sorry I .... (not write) for such a long time.
I .... (get) the letter you .... (send) me in July. Lots of things .... (happen) since then.

In August we .... (move) to our new house so we .... (be) very busy since then.
Sarah .... (phone) last Thursday and invited us to a party at her house on Friday.
We .... (go out) at seven but we .... (can not) find her house.
We .... (look for) over three hours before we .... (go) back home.

When we .... (go in) to our house Janet .... (turn on) the lights. Guess what?
There .... (be) nothing there. Burglars .... (come) and .... (take) everything while we .... (be) out.

The police .... (be) to the house lots of times since Friday but they still .... (not find) our things.

What a mess!

How are you?
What .... (do) since we last .... (see) you?

Please write soon,
Jack
   XX

8 Do the crossword.

What did you do yesterday? What have you done today?

Answers

Parts of the body II
page 4

1 1. forehead, 2. eyebrows, 3. eyelashes, 4. lips, 5. chin, 6. cheek

2 1. navel, 2. ankle, 3. beard, 4. thigh, 5. tongue, 6. armpit

3 1. lips – thinner, 2. beard – longer, 3. eyelashes – curlier, 4. moustache – pointier, 5. forehead – more wrinkled

4 1. pointiest, 2. curliest, 3. reddest, 4. smelliest, 5. most flexible

5 1. ankle, 2. chin, 3. forehead, 4. armpit, 5. moustache, 6. beard, 7. tongue, 8. thigh; 9. wrist

6 1. e, 2. c, 3. f, 4. h, 5. a, 6. g, 7. b, 8. d

7 c

8 moustache, eyelashes, wrist, elbow, armpit, lips, beard, eyebrows, forehead, tongue, ankle, navel, chest, thigh, heel: Something you are not good at doing is called your *Achille's* heel.

First aid
page 10

1 1. d, 2. a, 3. e, 4. b, 5. f, 6. g, 7. h, 8. c

2 1. bandage, 2. bruise, 3. plaster, 4. sling, 5. blood, 6. medicine

3 1. Chris had a cough. 2. Did Tony have a cold? 3. Michelle had a stomach ache. 4. Did you have a temperature?

4 1. Yes, she had a headache. 2. No, there wasn't much blood. 3. No, he didn't have a temperature. 4. Yes, it was sore. 5. Yes, his bruises were big. 6. Yes, they had sunburn. 7. No, I didn't have a toothache.

5 temperature, medicine, bandage, blood, toothache, headache, cough, cold: If someone is healthy we can say they are as *fit* as a *fiddle*.

6 1. Mrs Brown had a cough.
2. Her son, Jimmy, had a stomach ache.
3. Susan Power was on holiday and she had sunburn. 4. Mr Wilson had a toothache. 5. The twins had colds.
6. And me? At the end of the day I had a headache.

7 1. temperature, 2. blood, 3. medicine, 4. toothache, 5. hospital, 6. sling

8 1. stomach ache, 2. hospital, 3. nurse, 4. ambulance, 5. sling, 6. sore throat, 7. doctor, 8. plaster, 9. sunburn, 10. bruise, 11. medicine, 12. temperature, 13. cough, 14. chemist, 15. blood, 16. headache, 17. cold, 18. toothache, 19. bandage

How much?
page 16

1 1. c: ounce, 2. a: pound, 3. b: stone

2 1. d, 2. a, 3. f, 4. e, 5. g, 6. c, 7. b

3 1. There's a little rice but there are lots of potatoes. 2. There are a few biscuits but there's lots of chocolate. 3. There's a little bread but there's a lot of jam. 4. There is a little water but there are lots of cans.

5 1/2 pound, 6 ounces, 4 tablespoons, 1/4 teaspoon; 1. c, 2. b, 3. a, 4. d

6 1. a can of cola, 2. a tin of tuna, 3. a pound of flour, 4. a packet of pasta, 5. a tube of toothpaste, 6. a carton of juice, 7. a jar of strawberry jam, 8. a loaf of bread

7 1. bottle, 2. tin, 3. tea bag, 4. jar, 5. tube

8 1. box, 2. slice, 3. bottle, 4. teaspoon, 5. bar, 6. stone, 7. carton, 8. pound, 9. packet, 10. tea bag, 11. scales, 12. ounce, 13. dessertspoon, 14. tube, 15. jar, 16. tin, 17. loaf, 18. can, 19. tablespoon

In the garden   page 22

1 1. iris, 2. violet, 3. rose, 4. daisy, 5. sunflower, 6. tulip: "My *love* is like a red, red rose."

2 1. fir, 2. oak, 3. birch, 4. weeping willow, 5. cypress, 6. chestnut; You find lots of these trees in a *forest*.

3 1. What; They're yellow. 2. Where; They come from the Netherlands. 3. Why; Because Saint Valentine's Day is the feast of lovers. 4. When; They grow in summer.

4 1. Who gives you flowers? 2. What are your favourite flowers? 3. When do you get flowers? 4. Where do you buy flowers? 5. Why do you send flowers?

5 1. fir, 2. cypress, 3. chestnut, 4. weeping willow, 5. oak

6 1. sunflower, 2. daffodils, 3. daisy, daisies

7 1. daisy, 2. daffodil, 3. orchid, 4. violet, 5. tulip, 6. rose, 7. iris

8 daisies, roses, tulips, cyclamens, cypress, fir, weeping willow

9 weeping willow, cyclamen, iris, chestnut, snowdrop, daisy, violet, fir, tulip, sunflower, rose, daffodil, oak, birch, cypress, orchid: "*Trees* are *poems* that the *earth* writes upon the *sky*."

Cars   page 28

1 1. b, 2. d, 3. e, 4. f, 5. g, 6. c, 7. a

2 1. number plate, 2. boot, 3. windscreen, 4. door, 5. bumper, 6. steering wheel, 7. lights, 8. gear stick, 9. seat, 10. engine

3 1. turn on, lights; 2. take off, wheel; 3. wind up, window; 4. put on, seat belt; 5. press down, pedals; 6. looks in, rearview mirror

4 1. windscreen, 2. engine, 3. wheel, 4. light, 5. number plate

5 1. a, 2. b, 3. a, 4. b, 5. b, 6. b

6 1. b, 2. b, 3. b, 4. a

7 1. wheel, 2. boot, 2. jack, 4. horn

8 1. horn, 2. lights, 3. rearview mirror, 4. roof rack, 5. boot, 6. number plate, 7. windscreen, 8. door, 9. wheel,

10. engine, 11. steering wheel, 12. pedals, 13. gear stick, 14. bumper, 15. window, 16. windscreen wiper, 17. jack, 18. seat belt, 19. seat: *Henry Ford* made the first motor car in 1896.

Trains
page 34

1 1. passenger, 2. seat, 3. sleeping berth, 4. buffet, 5. tracks, 6. carriage

2 1. ticket office, 2. train, 3. ticket, 4. tracks, 5. sleeping berth, 6. platform

3 1. to, 2. in, 3. on, 4. from, 5. on, 6. in, on, 7. at, 8. in, 9. on, 10. in

4 1. on, train, 2. at, platform, 3. to, ticket collector, 4. in, left luggage, 5. at, buffet, 6. on, seat, 7. out of, window

5 1. trolley, 2. ticket office, 3. timetable, 4. waiting room, 5. sleeping berth, 6. left luggage

6 1. ticket office, 2. timetable, 3. left luggage, 4. waiting room, 5. sleeping car, 6. ticket gate, 7. carriage, 8. trolley, 9. tracks, 10. platform

7 1. b, 2. a

8 1. sleeping car, 2. sleeping berth, 3. buffet, 4. trolley, 5. train, 6. left luggage, 7. ticket, 8. ticket gate, 9. ticket office, 10. ticket collector, 11. window, 12. timetable, 13. seat, 14. passenger, 15. tracks, 16. carriage, 17. waiting room, 18. platform

Flying
page 40

1 aeroplane, runway, wing, gate, luggage, pilot, aisle, passport: The name of the very first aeroplane is *Flyer One*.

2 1. control tower, 2. runway, 3. gate, 4. aeroplane, 5. luggage, 6. baggage reclaim, 7. metal detector, 8. check-in

3 1. is about to/is going to land, 2. is going to apologize, 3. am about to/am going to fasten my seat belt, 4. are about to load, 5. will take off, 6. is going to/will miss

4 1. d: check-in, 2. c: boarding card, 3. g: metal detector, 4. b: gate, 5. a: passport, 6. e: seat belt, 7. f: aeroplane

5 1. flight attendant, 2. boarding card, 3. metal detector, 4. baggage reclaim

6 1. luggage, 2, window, aisle, 3. boarding card, 4. passport, 5. seat belts, 6. seat

7 1. c, 2. f, 3. d, 4. e, 5. b, 6. a

8 1. runway, 2. pilot, 3. aeroplane, 4. wing, 5. window, 6. flight attendant, 7. control tower

Hotels
page 46

1 1. conference room, 2. restaurant, 3. swimming pool, 4. reception, 5. lobby, 6. bar, 7. car park, 8. porter, 9. gym

2 1. single room, 2. twin room, 3. double room

3 1. Could/May, 2. Would, 3. May, 4. Could/May, 5. Would, 6. Could/May, 7. Could/Would, 8. Could

5 1. I would like a single room and full board, please. 2. Could I have a room with a view, please? 3. I would like a double room for next weekend, please.

91

4. Could I have air conditioning, please?
5. Could you ask the porter, please?
6. Could you please go to reception?
7. I would like the key to room 132.
8. Could I use the conference room, please?

6 1. reception, 2. twin room, 3. half board, 4. restaurant, 5. lobby, 6. full board

7 1. single rooms, 2. minibar, air conditioning, 3. half board, full board, 4. reception, 5. bar, restaurant, 6. swimming pool, 7. conference room, 8. car park

8 1. car park, 2. air conditioning, 3. single room, 4. minibar, 5. conference room, 6. porter

9 air conditioning, double room, gym, conference room, lobby, half board, bar, reception, porter, car park, restaurant, minibar, twin room, single room, swimming pool, full board, key: In *the Ormond Quay Hotel* in Dublin, James Joyce wrote some of his masterpiece *Ulysses*.

Music   page 52

1 1. score, 2. band, 3. concert, 4. saxophone, 5. CD, 6. note

2 saxophone, piano, keyboard, drums, violin, flute, cello, trumpet, accordion: They are all musical *instruments*.

3 1. played, drums, 2. played, band, 3. played, violin, 4. played, cello

4 1. violin, 2. trumpet, 3. double-bass, 4. conductor, 5. score, 6. flute

5 1. concert, 2. band, 3. CD, 4. conductor, 5. rock group, 6. flute

6 1. classical, 2. opera, 3. rock, 4. pop, 5. jazz, 6. blues, 7. rap, 8. folk

7 1. d, 2. c, 3. e, 4. b, 5. a

8 1. conductor, 2. double-bass, 3. score, 4. CD, 5. drums, 6. concert, 7. singer, 8. rock group, 9. trumpet, 10. piano, 11. orchestra, 12. accordion, 13. cello, 14. violin, 15. guitar, 16. note, 17. keyboard, 18. flute, 19. saxophone, 20. band

Films and plays   page 58

1 1. seat, 2. film, 3. gallery, 4. stage, 5. curtain: *Hamlet* is a famous play by Shakespeare.

2 1. director, 2. film, 3. screen, 4. stalls, 5. poster, 6. box office, 7. gallery: *Matrix* is a famous science-fiction trilogy.

3 1. Yes, she did. 2. No, he didn't. 3. No, I didn't. 4. Yes, they did. 5. No, they didn't.

4 1. Did they sit in the gallery? 2. Did you sit in front of the curtain? 3. Did he sit in the stalls?

5 1. box office, 2. stage, 3. poster, 4. curtain, 5. screen, 6. box

6 1. gallery, 2. poster, 3. ticket, 4. director: Actors say "*Break a leg*" before they go on stage.

7 1. box, 2. curtain, 3. stage, 4. actor, 5. stalls, 6. seat

8 1. seat, 2. stage, 3. screen, 4. director, 5. stalls, 6. ticket, 7. actress, 8. box, 9. gallery, 10. actor, 11. poster, 12. film, 13. box office, 14. curtain

Television

page 64

1 1. television set, 2. remote control, 3. DVD player, 4. videotape: *Telly* is a popular word for television.

2 documentary, cartoon, game show, talk show, news, film: *Soap operas are* television programmes with lots of episodes.

3 1. read, TV guide, 2. saw, film, 3. gave, DVD player, 4. bought, television set, 5. thought, documentary, 6. had, videotapes

4 1. d, 2. g, 3. f, 4. c, 5. h, 6. e, 7. a, 8. b

5 1. remote control, 2. video recorder, 3. TV guide, 4. aerial

6 1. news, 2. sports programme, 3. weather forecast, 4. cartoons, 5. documentaries, 6. films, 7. game shows, 8. talk show, 9. commercials

7 1. commercial, 2. TV guide, 3. remote control, 4. documentary, 5. film, 6. aerial, 7. talk show, 8. video recorder, 9. sports programme, 10. television set, 11. news, 12. weather forecast, 13. cartoon, 14. videotape, 15. game show, 16. DVD player

Technology

page 70

1 Music: car radio, hi-fi, CD player, Walkman, radio; **Communications:** mobile phone, fax, telephone, radio; **Other:** camcorder, calculator

2 a. 2, b. 5, c. 1, d. 7, e. 4, f. 8, g. 3, h. 6

3 1. were, mobile phone, 2. was, computer, 3. were, fax, 4. was, photocopier, 5. was, Walkman, CD player

4 1. car radio, 2. mobile phone, telephone, 3. laptop, 4. camera

5 1. hi-fi, 2. CD player, 3. calculator, 4. answering machine, 5. scanner, 6. car radio, 7. satellite dish

6 1. e, 2. g, 3. f, 4. b, 5. a, 6. c, 7. d

7 1. filmed, 2. printed, 3. faxed, 4. took photos, 5. scanned, 6. texted, 7. photocopied

8 At home/at work: telephone, computer, fax, scanner, hi-fi, answering machine, photocopier, printer, satellite dish; **in the car:** car radio; **elsewhere:** mobile phone, camera, camcorder, CD player/Discman, calculator, radio, Walkman

9 1. car radio, 2. printer, 3. telephone, 4. camera, 5. fax, 6. satellite dish, 7. Walkman, 8. hi-fi, 9. scanner, 10. laptop, 11. calculator, 12. answering machine, 13. mobile phone, 14. computer, 15. camcorder, 16. CD player, 17. radio, 18. photocopier

Sport II

page 76

1 1. high jump, 2. long jump, 3. hurdles; decathlon: These three sports are all part of the *Decathlon*. There are ten events in the decathlon.

2 1. f, 2. g, 3. e, 4. c, 5. a, 6. d, 7. b

3 1. Yes, they've played squash. / Yes, they have. 2. No, he has never watched American football. / No, he hasn't watched American football. 3. Have you ever tried skateboarding? 4. Have you ever played table tennis?

4 American football, baseball, rowing, ice hockey: They're all *team sports*.

5 1. boxing, 2. long jump, 3. windsurfing, 4. high jump, 5. diving, 6. weightlifting, 7. skateboarding, 8. squash, 9. karate, 10. hurdles: They are all *individual* sports.

6 Races: bobsleighing, rowing, hurdles; **Games:** squash, American football, ice hockey, baseball, table tennis; **Performance-based:** windsurfing, skateboarding, diving, karate; **Tests of strength:** weightlifting, boxing

7 1. high jump, 2. long jump, 3. hurdles

8 1. weightlifting, 2. windsurfing, 3. baseball, 4. squash, 5. diving, 6. bobsleighing, 7. high jump, 8. motorcycling, 9. hurdles, 10. skateboarding, 11. boxing, 12. karate, 13. table tennis, 14. long jump, 15. ice hockey, 16. American football, 17. rowing

Daily actions   page 82

1 1. f, 2. d, 3. c, 4. g, 5. i, 6. h, 7. e, 8. a, 9. b

2 1. put on make-up, 2. go up, 3. take, 4. go in, 5. wave, 6. wash up: Things you do every day are part of your *routine*.

3 1. she's sent, 2. waited for, 3. turned on, 4. hasn't finished

4 1. find, 2. go up, 3. go in, 4. turn on

5 1. When Luke went in he turned on the light. 2. I sorry I haven't written for a long time. 3. Have you paid all your bills? 4. She put on her make-up before she went out. 5. They waved when they went into the bus. 6. I have never written a poem.

7 I haven't written, got, sent, have happened, moved, have been, phoned, went out, couldn't, looked for, went, went in, turned on, was, came, took, were, have been, haven't found, have you done, saw

8 1. find, 2. wait for, 3. write, 4. go out, 5. go in, 6. clean, 7. look for, 8. turn off, 9. take, 10. turn on, 11. go up, 12. wave, 13. pay, 14. go down, 15. phone, 16. wash up, 17. put on make-up, 18. send

Contents

Parts of the body II	page 4
First aid	10
How much?	16
In the garden	22
Cars	28
Trains	34
Flying	40
Hotels	46
Music	52
Films and plays	58
Television	64
Technology	70
Sport II	76
Daily actions	82
Answers	89